Varieties of Magic Realism

Dr. Clark Zlotchew

Academic Press ENE

Copyright © Clark Zlotchew
Academic Press ENE
All rights reserved.
No part of this publication may be reproduced, stored in a retrieval system, or transmitted, in any form or by any means (electronic, mechanical, photocopying, recording or otherwise), without the prior written permission of both, the copyright owner and the publisher of this book.
Ediciones Nuevo Espacio – Academic Press ENE
New Jersey, 07704, USA
http://www.editorial-ene.com
AcademicPressENE@aol.com
First Edition, March, 2007
ISBN: 1-930879-47-4

About the Author

Clark M. Zlotchew, Ph.D., has been a professor of Spanish language and linguistics and of the literatures of Spain and of Spanish America at SUNY College at Fredonia since 1975.

He received his Master of Arts degree in Spanish from Middlebury College (Vermont) and his Ph.D. in Romance Languages and Literatures from SUNY Binghamton. Professor Zlotchew has had more than a dozen books published, ranging from literary criticism to translations of Spanish and Spanish-American short fiction and poetry, to interviews with writers of Argentina and Uruguay.

He is also the author, under a pen name, of a military/action novel. Dr. Zlotchew has had numerous articles published in prestigious journals on Spanish and Spanish-American literature, as well as on Hispanic dialectology, and has presented papers on these subjects on four continents.

Acknowledgements

Chapter 1 has appeared in Spanish and in different form as "El manipulador manipulado: El determinismo ajedrecista en Borges," *KaÑina:Revista de Artes y Letras de la Universidad de Costa Rica*, 10, 2 (Julio-diciembre, 1986), 29-33.
Chapter 2 has appeared, in different form, as "Tlon, Llhuros, N. Daly, J. L. Borges," *Modern Fiction Studies*, 19, 3 (Autumn 1973), 453-59.
Chapter 3 has appeared in somewhat different form as "Fiction Wrapped in Fiction: Causality in Borges and the *Nouveau Roman*, " *Inti: Revista de Literatura Hispánica*, 15 (Primavera, 1982), 25-32.
Chapter 4 has appeared, in Spanish and in somewhat different form, as "La experiencia directa de la obsesiva fantasía en Borges y en Robbe-Grillet," *KáÑina:Revista de Artes y Letras de la Universidad de Costa Rica*, 4, 1 (enero-junio 1980), 61-67.
Chapter 5 has appeared in Spanish, and in different form, in "El lector como escritor en Borges y en Robbe-Grillet," *Letras de Buenos Aires*, año 5, No. 14 (December 1985), 15-20.
Chapter 7 has appeared in different form in "Utopian Escapism in Julio Ricci: Golden Age Transmuted into Geography," *Inti: Revista de Literatura Hispánica*, 24-25 (Fall 1986-Spring 1987), 145-154.
Some of the material of Chapter 9, in a very different form, appeared as "Antonio Brailovsky, Magic Realism and the Twentieth-Century Inquisition," *Jewish Affairs*, 53, 1 (Autumn 1998), 25-29.
Chapter 10 has appeared in Spanish and in different form as "Metáforas de la creación literaria en tres cuentos de Enrique Jaramillo Levi," *Alba de América: Revista Literaria*, 8, 14-15 (1990), 141-48.

Introduction: Toward A Definition Of Magic Realism	9
Chapter 1 Borges: Man As Instrument	31
Chapter 2 Borges: Magic Realism In Real Life	47
Chapter 3 Borges And The French "New Novel": Fiction Wrapped In Fiction	61
Chapter 4 Borges And The French "New Novel": The Unmediated Experience	73
Chapter 5 Borges And The French "New Novel": The Reader As Accomplice	87
Chapter 6 Carlos Fuentes' *Aura*: Magic, Sex And Destiny	99
Chapter 7 Julio Riccl: Time Transmuted Into Space	109
Chapter 8 Julio Ricci: Return To Eden	123
Chapter 9 Antonio Brailovsky: Beneath The Surface Of Reality	145
Chapter 10 Enrique Jaramillo Levi: Magical Metaphors Of Literary Creativity	157
Notes	169

INTRODUCTION
TOWARD A DEFINITION OF MAGIC REALISM

> There are more things in heaven and earth, Horatio, than are dreamt of in your philosophy.
> Shakespeare (*Hamlet*), I, v, 166.

The term "magic realism" (or "magical realism") has been bruited about with great frequency in the last half of the twentieth century, especially with reference to contemporary Latin American literature, yet it is not always clear exactly what is meant by this designation. The expression "magic realism" would seem to be an oxymoron, since "realism" in literature is thought of as an imitation or reflection of real life --bound by all the physical rules of nature with which we are familiar-- whereas "magic" is something quite different, something that shatters or reverses or transcends those rules.

"Magic," after all, is the word we assign to any procedure that supposedly enables a human being to exercise control over the forces of nature or over supernatural agencies. When a human being does this, the process is called "magic," or "witchcraft" or "sorcery" or "enchantment." When the laws of nature are suspended by a supernatural force, however, the same resultant phenomenon is termed a "miracle." For example, the Bible recounts that God parted the Red Sea for the Israelites; this is a miracle. Had Moses, a human being, effectuated the same feat by means of his own power, his own control over natural or divine forces, it would be termed "magic." But magic realism, which has a great deal to do with realism, does not necessarily concern "magic" as defined above.

To further obfuscate the issue, magic realism is often confused or used interchangeably with terms such as "the fantastic," "the uncanny," "the marvelous," "marvelous reality" "the supernatural" and "surrealism." Yet, literary critics have attempted to separate these terms and define the kinds of literature they represent. As might be expected, total consensus has remained elusive, while polemics abound. A review of the history of the term "magic realism" would be helpful. More importantly, an examination of definitions of magic realism and the various other literary modes with which it is often confused would provide orientation in this field, although the prospect of disorientation cannot be discounted.

HISTORY: As Víctor Bravo mentions (p. 14), Felix Welht had already employed the term "magic realism" ("Magische Realismus" in German) in referring to the literary work of Franz Kafka, a Czech Jew who wrote in German a century ago. Dostoyevsky, the nineteenth-century Russian novelist, used a similar term to describe his own technique: "fantastic realism" (Víctor Bravo, Ibid.). The term "realismo mágico" ("magic realism") was introduced into the Spanish language from German with the Spanish translation of a book --not on Latin American literature, but on European painting-- by Franz Roh. Roh's book dealt with a new Post Expressionist phase of painting which had developed in Europe and the United States at the close of World War I.

The term was appropriated by Arturo Uslar Pietri in 1948, more than two decades after having read the Spanish version of Franz Roh's book, to refer to the Venezuelan short story from the 1920s to his own day.

> Lo que vino a predominar en el cuento [venezolano] y a marcar su huella de una manera perdurable fue la consideración del hombre como misterio en medio de datos realistas. Una adivinación poética o una negación poética de la realidad. Lo que a falta de otra palabra podrá llamarse un realismo mágico. ("El cuento..." p. 287).

> What has come to predominate in the [Vene-

zuelan] short story and to leave a lasting mark was the consideration of man as a mystery in the midst of realistic data. A poetic divination or a poetic negation of reality. What, lacking any other word, could be called a magical realism.

In 1949 Cuban writer Alejo Carpentier used the term "lo real maravilloso" ("marvelous [or 'wondrous'] reality") on introducing his novel *El reino de este mundo* (*The Kingdom of This World*), later applying the term to his subsequent works as well. Carpentier's meaning is that [Latin] America itself --its geography, its history, its people and their myths and beliefs-- is wondrous, literally marvelous, i.e. filled with marvels. In this way, writing about this land automatically produces a literature of marvelous reality.

The terms magic realism and marvelous reality, are difficult to separate and differentiate; they have a great deal in common. Many critics have used the terms interchangeably. However, one difference lies in the focus. The term magic realism refers to the fictional world created by the writer, whereas marvelous reality, in theory, refers to the supposedly real world of Latin America --a world of marvels-- that the writer simply portrays in his/her fiction.

Angel Flores, in 1955, fixes the year 1935 as the birth date of magic realism, including under this rubric the most disparate Latin American writers. This general idea is continued by Luis Leal in 1967. Uslar Pietri, in 1969, expands his earlier definition of magic realism to include both Cuban writer Alejo Carpentier and Guatemalan writer Miguel Ángel Asturias. He mentions that many critics believe there are surrealistic elements in these writers, but adds that a rebirth of baroque forms can be found in them as well, in addition to "un peculiar modo de rea- lismo que han dado en llamar realismo mágico" ("a peculiar brand of realism that is being called magical realism.") ("De Amadís..." p. 56).

In his essay of 1985, "Realismo mágico," Uslar Pietri broadens even further his understanding of the term "magic realism," linking it to conditions peculiar to Latin America,[1] adding that these conditions are impossible to reduce to any European model. This is the understanding of magic realism evinced by many Latin American writers and critics at present.

Many of these Latin American critics and fiction writers tend to lump various manifestations of Latin American literature together as examples of magic realism if two factors are present: (1) the narrative is not limited strictly to a mirroring of objective reality, and (2) the author happens to be Latin American.

The first factor is extremely broad and all-encompassing, allowing for the fuzzy perception of all forms of fantasy, the uncanny, the marvelous (or wondrous), the supernatural, the surreal and anything else which is not one-hundred percent reality-based. The second factor is highly restrictive; it automatically excludes works written by Europeans, Anglo-Americans, or anyone else who is not Latin American.

The reasoning behind this attitude is that in Latin American culture, and therefore in its literature, there is a blend of European logic and scientific attitude ("rationality") with indigenous superstition and acceptance of the supernatural as a normal feature of life ("irrationality"). As we shall see, this blend of the so-called "rational" with the "irrational" is part of the definition of magic realism. Hence, according to this rationale, Latin American thought is, by definition, an expression of magic realism, and vice-versa. However, a literary term based, not on the examination of literary themes and techniques, but on the nationality of the writer, tends to be almost useless as a definition of a literary mode.

There is no doubt that confusion and contradiction are involved in any discussion of magic realism. This can be appreciated in comparing the opinions of just two Latin American literary critics. On one hand, Angel Flores not only includes Jorge Luis Borges (as well as Ernesto Sábato, and a heterogeneous list of many other writers) among the magical realists, but goes so far as to date magic realism itself from the year in which Borges published his *Historia universal de la infamia* (1935). On the other hand, Lucila-Inés Mena doubts that Borges (as well as Ernesto Sábato, Julio Cortázar and Carlos Fuentes) can even be included among the magic realists (Mena, p. 407). These are not isolated opinions.

Borges is often regarded as the leading magical realist. The view that Borges is not a magical realist (sometimes, not even quite Latin American) is fairly common among an entire school of Latin American writers and critics; this is mainly because the Argentinean author is seen as too "European," his work as lacking indigenous inspiration, or because his production too often reflects urban rather than rural life. These contradictory attitudes seem to be the result of two different sets of criteria. The Borges-as-magic realist stance is based on strictly literary criteria, and is therefore more convincing than the attitude reflecting ethno-socio-cultural standards.

(In passing, it should be noted that there is a general, only half-joking, tendency in Latin America to consider Argentina itself outside the "truly" Latin American fold. There is a saying in some Latin American circles which rhymes nicely in Spanish: "La América Latina/ termina/en la Argentina" ("Latin America ends at Argentina"). This reflects a racially as well as culturally based concept: Argentineans are too European, not sufficiently mestizo.)

At this point, the tracing of the history of the term "magic realism" has brought us up to the present and to the question of definition, with which it is inextricably entwined.

DEFINITIONS: It would be helpful to state first what magic realism is not, in order to separate it conceptually from the modes of literature which are often confused with it. It is not synonymous with the fantastic, although it may share some of its ingredients.

In the fantastic there are two dimensions: the realistic, rational, everyday world governed by the laws of nature as we have been taught them, on one hand, and the mysterious, irrational, supernatural world we are unable to comprehend. In this bidimensional world, the irrational and unfamiliar seem to break in upon the rational and familiar. An important element of the fantastic is the surprise and even fear experienced by the implied author and/or protagonist upon confronting the irrational. The reader shares this astonishment and/or anxiety, but cannot decide whether the events (or the situation) are caused by supernatural powers or have a rational explication. Neither can the implied author.

The fantastic, according to Tzvetan Todorov, is "that hesitation experienced by a person who knows only the laws of nature, confronting an apparently supernatural event" (Todorov, p. 25). Todorov also quotes the definition of the fantastic provided by nineteenth-century Russian philosopher and mystic, Vladimir Solovyov: "In the genuine fantastic, there is always the external and formal possibility of a simple explanation of phenomena, but at the same time this explanation is completely stripped of internal probability" (Ibid. pp. 25-26). Todorov clarifies by adding, "there is an uncanny phenomenon which we can explain in two fashions, by types of natural causes and supernatural causes. The possibility of a hesitation between the two creates the fantastic effect" (Ibid. p. 26).

It is this "hesitation" between the attribution of natural or supernatural causes to a peculiar and unsettling phenomenon, between rational and irrational explanations, that defines the fantastic.

Todorov's mention of an "uncanny phenomenon" brings us to a definition of the accepted English term, "the uncanny," with reference to a mode of writing that Todorov considers a genre related to the fantastic, but different from it.[2] Amaryll Beatrice Chanady explains that the "uncanny can be produced either by mysterious happenings that turn out to have natural causes, or by the presence of something that is generally disquieting" (Chanady, p. 4).[3]

The difference between the fantastic and the uncanny, then, is that in the former the protagonist (and implied author) cannot decide whether the extraordinary situation or event has supernatural origins or a perfectly natural explanation; he/she is left hanging between the two possibilities. In the uncanny, on the other hand, either there is merely an uncomfortable feeling about some presence in the fiction, without that "presence" being explicitly supernatural, or it is understood at some point that the peculiar situation is definitely not supernatural, but has a rational explanation.

A related mode is "the marvelous." In the marvelous, there is no question of uncanny or supernatural events intruding on the familiar, rational, logical world the reader has been taught to accept. There is but one dimension in the world of the marvelous. In this monodimensional world anything can happen without surprising the implied author, because the entire world of the marvelous is filled with beings and situations we would normally consider to be supernatural. Magic is the normal and expected milieu of the marvelous world.

Fairy tales belong to the marvelous mode. The characters in a fairy tale are not at all surprised to encounter witches, trolls or monsters, or to find people placed under magic spells (Chanady, pp. 2-3). The monodimensional marvelous is very different from the bidimensional world of the fantastic, in which the possibility of the supernatural intrudes upon the familiar universe, producing a shock.

Another mode of writing (and painting) possessing points of contact with magic realism has been labeled "surrealism." Surrealism began with a group of writers and painters working in Paris between the two World Wars. Clustered around the poet André Breton, they adopted a positive philosophy inspired by the psychological theories of Sigmund Freud. Believing that society repressed man's true nature, they felt that in both life and art it was imperative to allow full freedom to the imagination. Breton, in his *First Surrealist Manifesto* (1924) defined surrealism as "pure psychic automatism," and proclaimed that it was to be accomplished by writing without conscious control.

In practice, surrealism attempts to transfer to the page (or the canvass) the highly symbolic processes stemming directly from the unconscious without passing through the conscious mind. Dreams, as Freud has shown, stem from the unconscious and "speak" in highly symbolic images which to the conscious mind seem unreal, magical, illogical and mysterious. This explains the highly oneiric quality of surrealistic works.

There is also a strong connection with myth in surrealism, because myths as well as dreams appear to originate in the unconscious. Jungian psychologists find that many of the symbols and themes found in fairy tales and myths are the same as those detected in the dreams of modern patients and stem from identical fears and needs.[4] This phenomenon was noted by Freud in his patients as well. A familiar example is the myth of Oedipus and the Freudian complex named for it.

Now that we have seen what magic realism is not -- or at least some of the things it is not-- but that are closely associated with it, with some trepidation we shall enter the minefield of what it actually is. Trepidation because, as one recent critic put it, "Existe controversia y confusión al respecto [definir el realismo mágico] y aún no se cuenta con una acepción que tenga aceptación general" ("Controversy and confusion exists in this matter [defining magic realism] and there is still no definition that has been universally accepted.") (Bautista Gutiérrez, p. 13).

A great many critics believe, as we have seen, that magic realism is the result of the blend of European logical-scientific rationality and the autochthonous New World's primitive, mythical, magical and superstitious irrationality. Furthermore, they believe that the Latin American writers who are considered magic realists reflect this duality in their writings.

It is ironic that so many Latin American critics believe this and think that they themselves, the critics, are the product of the culture thus described. At times it appears to be a misplaced pseudo-patriotism, even jingoism, by which the critics share in the glory of the writers by belonging to the same unique culture, the only one in the world that shares features of European and Native American cultures.

Fairly recently, Gloria Bautista Gutiérrez naively exaggerated this concept to the point at which the magic realist writer becomes, in her estimation, a socially-conscious paladin of the Hispanic people: "En general, diríase que la narrativa mágicorrealista presenta una especie de solidaridad entre el escritor [hispanoamericano] y su pueblo" ("In general, one would say that the magical realist narrative presents a kind of solidarity between the [Spanish American] writer and h/her people") (Bautista Gutiérrez, p. 39). The same statement could be made --and more convincingly-- about the highly realistic, unimaginative writings of many of the authors of the defunct Soviet Union. It is certainly more applicable to the Latin American social realists who were writing in the 1930s and 40s.

The irony lies in that the adjectives employed to describe the indigenous features of the thought patterns supposedly expressed by magic realist authors --"primitive"; "mythical"; "superstitious"; "irrational"-- tend to be demeaning, or at least condescending, and, more to the point, seem to indicate the viewpoint of the outsider. Those whose Weltanschauung could be described (by others) as "irrational" and "superstitious" would never describe their own world views with these patronizing adjectives; only an outsider would.

Not only the critics, but the magic realist authors themselves, more often than not are fascinated by the very exoticism, that is, otherness, they see in the "primitive" way of interpreting the world they portray. Neither the Latin American magic realists nor the critics who explain them (often they are one and the same person) see the world as the narrators and characters they invent do. People who do interpret reality in that "superstitious" manner do not write books, let alone the best sellers associated with the magic realists. Often they do not read or write at all. Once the so-called "primitive" becomes a writer of literature, if this were to happen, h/she has entered the world of the written word, which in Latin America means words written in Spanish or Portuguese --European languages-- and ceases to think in the patterns described on the pages of the magic realists.

In this light, it is interesting to note Lucila-Inés Mena's statement concerning magic realism:

> También es notable el hecho de que aquellos autores a quienes más comúnmente se denomina mágicorrealistas cultivan una temática que enfoca insistentemente la realidad americana a través de sus mitos y de su naturaleza primigenia. Podríamos pensar entonces que el uso de lo maravilloso que esta realidad proporciona sea uno de los factores que nos lleva a considerar a Rulfo, Carpentier, Asturias y García Márquez como escritores mágicorrealistas, mientras dudamos acerca de la filiación magicorrealista de Borges, Cortázar, Sábato y Fuentes (Mena, p. 407).

> It is also notable that those authors who are most commonly designated as magical realists cultivate themes that insistently focus on the American reality through its myths and its primeval nature. We could then think that the use of the marvelous that this reality provides may be one of the factors that leads us to consider Rulfo, Carpentier, Asturias and García Márquez to be magic realist writers, while we hesitate concerning the magic realist affiliation of Borges, Cortázar, Sábato and Fuentes.

Alejo Carpentier was raised in Cuba, a land in which the indigenous culture was completely exterminated 500 years ago, but in which a vigorous culture of Spanish and African origins subsists. He is of French and Russian parents, and received his education in Europe and the United States. A talented, urbane and sophisticated musicologist imbued with European tradition and aware of its mythology, Carpentier is neither superstitious nor "primitive" (whatever this adjective means). But even those without European parentage --who probably do spring from mestizo origins, sharing the genetic heritage of both Europeans and American natives, and who are mentioned by Mena, along with Carpentier, as magic realists-- are no more superstitious or "primitive" than the cosmopolitan Carpentier. Asturias, the magic realist par excellence, wrote much of his magic realism while living in Paris.

While these writers may cultivate the themes mentioned by Mena, they do so as outsiders, in much the same way that some Europeans writers indulged in what is usually called exoticism, or the way that Rubén Darío -- Nicaraguan-born Modernist-- wrote of China and Japan and blue-eyed European princesses. The magic realists are fascinated by the exotic --I translate: the alien-- qualities of the thought patterns they seek to represent. The fact that the writers proceed from lands in which these patterns once were the only patterns, and where in many cases they still subsist among large sectors of the rural population, is not the reason they write as they do.

Conversely, a European or North American or any writer not born in Latin America, but who writes in a certain manner (still to be defined) can be just as much a magic realist as the Latin American author who satisfies the same requisites. In this light, it is instructive to note the contradictions in Ángel Flores's statements that, on one hand, magic realism is an "auténtica expresión" ("authentic expression") of Latin America (Flores, p. 192), and, on the other hand, that he finds the roots of magical realism in Kafka and Proust (Ibid. p. 188), two very European Jews who wrote in German and French respectively.

Part of the evidence that the magic realists and the critics who define magic realism from the ethnocentric point of view write from without rather than within the mentality supposedly reflected in magic realism, is their assigning all the logic, science and rationality to the European influence, while reserving the myth, superstition and irrationality for the indigenous factors. This, ironically, is in itself a Eurocentric viewpoint.

The European tradition of logical thought and scientific inquiry, after all, subsists in conjunction with Pagan mythologies and the Christian religion, belief patterns based, not on logic or scientific observation, but on faith, which is the belief in what cannot be seen or weighed or measured. The Second Coming of Christ is no more logical or scientific than the Aztecs' belief in the return of the god Quetzalcóatl; both are matters of faith. Certainly, indigenous American superstition --e.g. nahualism among the Guatemalan Indians-- is no more irrational than the European belief in ghosts, vampires, werewolves, witches or leprechauns.[5]

The position of those Latin American critics who assert that magic realism is a current within literature that is universal, and not limited to any region or ethnos, seems a more literarily promising stance. As Valbuena Briones puts it:

> El realismo mágico no se limita, como ha creído algún crítico, a los pueblos latinoamericanos que tengan una amplia población de indios y negros y que con sus culturas pueden presentar una nueva realidad en la que se funden elementos irracionales y primitivos, sino que... es una corriente universal, y se puede añadir que inherente al ser humano. (Valbuena Briones, p. 236).

> Magic realism is not limited, as some critic would have it, to the Latin American peoples that have a substantial population of Indians and Blacks and who with their cultures can present a new reality in which irrational and primitive elements are fused, but that... it is a universal current, and, one might add, inherent in human beings.

As we have seen, starting with Uslar Pietri in the forties, "magic realism" became a term that purported to represent the true nature of the (Latin) American world view. However, nationality or ethnicity is at best an external, tangential means of classifying a literary mode. A more internal, central, and therefore more serviceable method, is an analysis of the technical and thematic concerns present in the mode under study. According to Chanady, magic realism (like the fantastic) is a "literary mode, rather than a specific, historically identifiable genre, and can be found in most types of prose fiction" (Chanady, pp. 16-17). For Roberto González Echevarría, the term is used to identify "moments" of art and literature that are completely different one from the other (González Echevarría, pp. 19-22).

The term is now used by many writers and critics to describe the technical procedures and thematic interests of various authors. Chanady admits, "The concept is extremely vague and refers to three distinct activities --pictorial art, the expression of a national literature, and literary criticism" (Chanady, p. 17).

Precisely because of this lack of relationship or continuity among these three distinct activities, González Echevarría states that "magic realism lacks the cohesion necessary to be able to be considered a literary or critical movement" (González Echevarría, pp.22-23). Emir Rodríguez Monegal believes that the term has become so perplexing, often being applied to any Spanish American writer who is not "crasamente naturalista" ("crassly naturalistic"), that the designation should be abandoned altogether, since it strangles, rather than stimulates, critical dialogue (Rodríguez Monegal, p. 27).

Bautista Gutiérrez lists ten characteristics which can be attributed to magic realism (actually, they are more like fifteen crammed into 10 numbered categories) (pp. 38-39), yet most of the characteristics she lists are equally applicable to the literary modes most often confused with magic realism, while others refer to a preoccupation with the political, social and cultural problems of Latin America, elements found in literature that has nothing to do with magic realism.

Still others of these characteristics listed are so general that they could apply equally well to any kind of good literature at all (e.g. a precise and clear style). One of these characteristics, while typical of fantasy, even contradicts what separates fantasy from magic realism: "La sorpresa es el resultado de la combinación de factores reales o irreales, concretos o abstractos, trágicos y/o absurdos" ("The surprise is the result of the combination of factors that are real or unreal, concrete or abstract, tragic and/or absurd") (Bautista Gutiérrez, p. 38). The element of "surprise" belongs, as we have seen, to the fantastic, not to magic realism (nor the marvelous, in which the implied author is not surprised by the phenomena described, no matter how supernatural or unfamiliar they might seem to the rational reader). This list of characteristics, then, is not useful.

Although there is no consensus among critics as to what elements are basic to magic realism, certain features do seem to be typical. Perhaps the most obvious characteristic found in magic realism is the presence of the supernatural, which is to say, whatever processes cannot be explained by logical thought or our scientific experience with the real world. This supernatural element, however, in order to form part of magic realism, must be included within the framework of a rigorously realistic fictional world. So far, this condition applies equally well to both magic realism and the fantastic.

There is a difference, nevertheless, between these two related literary modes. The fantastic is typified by a hesitation on the part of the characters and the implied author --and, therefore, the reader-- between a supernatural cause and a rational explanation --what Chanady designates "unresolved antinomy" (subtitle and passim). Magic realism, on the contrary, involves the integration of two separate perspectives --the rational and the supernatural-- into one single system. In this system there is no hesitation. The presence of the supernatural causes no surprise to the protagonist or implied author, but rather is accepted as a totally normal and expected component of reality within the fiction.

In the fantastic the supernatural is problematic, while in magic realism it is not. Yet, as we have seen above, the supernatural or irrational is also regarded as perfectly normal in fairy tales and other forms of what has been designated the "marvelous."

One major difference between magic realism and the marvelous --without resorting to ethnicity-- is that the entire world of the marvelous, while "real" to the characters and the implied author, seems unreal to the reader; almost nothing seems a part of the normal world that exists outside the work of fiction. In magic realism, however, most of the fictional world seems very familiar and realistic to the reader while containing those unfamiliar and unreal (for the reader) elements that are part of the implied author's reality. In fact, what we are labeling "rational" and "irrational," "natural" and "supernatural," or "real" and "unreal," as the elements of a magical realist world, is bidimensional only for the reader and actual author.[6] For the characters and the implied author, these elements are all "natural" and normal factors of a monodimensional totality.

This attitude can be seen in some of the works of Borges. For example, in "Tlon, Uqbar, Orbis Tertius," a short story in *Ficciones*, for example, in which a secret society invents a fictional country, Uqbar, and places information on this country in an encyclopedia. Centuries later, the society expands its field of operations, inventing an entire planet, Tlon, and its civilizations, writing books and articles describing it.

Years later, objects made of unidentifiable substances are found in Buenos Aires, inscribed in one of the alphabets of Tlon. Borges notes that in the school system the history of Tlon is replacing the history he had been taught. He predicts that Spanish and English will disappear, replaced by the languages of Tlon. Borges, who is the implied as well as the true author of this story, relates these bizarre events with resignation rather than astonishment, regret rather than fear, in a matter-of-fact tone. This, certainly, responds to the strictest definitions of magic realism.

Borges never used the term "magic realism," but he has referred to "magic" as essential to literature. In his essay, "El arte narrativo y la magia," in the collection *Discusión*, first published in 1932, Borges refers, using the term "magic," to events in fiction which obey only the logic of the piece of fiction in which they are contained, rather than that of the outside world.[7] The events are made acceptable to the reader by what Borges calls "prophesying," i.e., foreshadowing, by dropping hints about what can happen in the world of the particular piece of fiction.

In early Europe people did not distinguish between objective reality and subjective interpretations of the world. This was a time in which people fully believed in what we now call myth. Today these myths may be familiar to us, and we may enjoy them, but we do not believe in them as objective truth. Carter Wheelock points out that nineteenth-century Realism so closely reflected the objective reality of the world outside the fictional work, that it gave rise to a "sub-class of 'minor' fiction called fantastic."

Wheelock credits Borges for re-combining the two poles, thus paving the way for a newer literature now typified as "imaginative, magically real, or mythic..." ("Borges, Cortázar, and the Aesthetic...", p. 4). Wheelock's article demonstrates that Borges's "magical causality" can be found in much of Cortázar's fiction as well, "in order to get at the aesthetic concept underlying the self-encapsulating literature that has repudiated realism" (Ibid. 3). In speaking of this kind of fiction, produced by Borges and Cortázar, Wheelock also uses the terms "magical reality" and the "new realism."

The Guatemalan magic realist, Miguel Ángel Asturias, views magic realism in the following way: "You can meet an Indian who describes to you how he has seen an enormous rock turn into a person, or a cloud turn into an enormous rock. This situation is a tangible reality which for the Indian involves an understanding of supernatural forces." [8] A situation that in the fantastic would amaze the implied author and unnerve the protagonist, in magic realism is accepted as a normal everyday occurrence. Unlike in fiction of the marvelous, e.g., a fairy tale, the portrayal of the supernatural in a work of magic realism, for example, as purportedly understood by the American native protagonist, takes place within a rigorously realistic narrative and, for the protagonist, is part of the natural world.

In a recent article, William Spindler sees three types of magic realism. His "metaphysical" magic realism concerns reality viewed in a manner that brings out its magical qualities. "Anthropological" magic realism is produced by a narrator who sometimes introduces phenomena from a strictly rational standpoint, and at times from a supernatural viewpoint. Spindler's third category, "ontological" magic realism presents the extraordinary as though it were ordinary. The last two categories appear to be no more than two different views of the same mode of literature; they both agree with Asturias' explanations above.

The attribution to the Native American mentality of an acceptance of supernatural forces --as in Asturias' explanation— is what prompts many writers to believe that magic realism is the exclusive property of Latin American writers. Yet this flat acceptance of that which is inexplicable and even impossible in the rational world, is exactly the situation we find, for instance, in the matter-of-fact description of a man awakening one morning to find himself converted into an insect in Kafka's *The Metamorphosis*. Neither the implied author nor any of the characters is amazed or particularly surprised by this transformation, which is treated practically as nothing more dismaying than waking up with a case of the flu.

If, then, we accept the view that one of the components of magic realism is that it is found exclusively in works written by Latin Americans, the writings of European and North American authors are automatically excluded from this literary mode. It would be more in keeping with literary analysis —more literarily valid— to remove this condition from the definition of magic realism. At the same time it should be recognized that magic realism has flourished to spectacular proportions in the Latin American fiction of the last half of the twentieth century.

Some critics see magic realism as a merging of the fantastic with the real, while others consider it to be the depiction of the mystery that lies within reality itself. It is this latter view (Spindler's "metaphysical" magic realism) that seems most convincing as an argument for magic realism as a category distinct from the others with which it is often confused. As an example of this latter view:

> ...lo que más comúnmente se ha dado en llamar realismo mágico consiste en una cierta penetración en la realidad, de parte de algunos autores, que hace que su cosmovisión sea más profunda, compleja y poética. Tal penetración en la realidad produce el desdoblamiento de ésta y se nos presenta entonces, no sólo el aspecto sensorial y objetivo de las cosas, sino también su lado oculto, ambiguo y misterioso (Mena, p. 401).
>
> ...what most commonly has been called magic realism consists of a certain insight into reality, on the part of some authors, who make their cosmovision deeper, more complex and poetic. Such insight into reality produces an opening up of reality, and we are then presented not only with the objective sensorial aspect of things, but also their hidden side, ambiguous and mysterious.

In line with the above idea is Antonio Brailovsky's description:

> Yo creo que la realidad generalmente es más fantástica que la ficción. Es decir, estamos acostumbrados a ver una parte menor de la realidad. Pero si nosotros somos capaces de percibir la realidad en su conjunto, entonces nos encontramos con cosas mu-

cho más desmesuradas que la magia. (Zlotchew, "Entrevista..." p. 379).

I believe that reality generally is more fantastic than fiction. That is, we are accustomed to seeing one part, a minor part, of reality. But if we are capable of perceiving reality completely, as a whole, then we find ourselves among things much more extreme than magic. (Zlotchew, *Voices*, p. 61.)

The idea that truth is stranger than fiction, were the whole truth perceived, lies at the core of magic realism. Put another way, magic realism can stem from a highly subjective observation of the real world. It is perceived reality filtered through the imagination, or reality undergoing interpretation and expressed metaphorically. While recognizing that magic realism --in its many variants-- has been a major factor in Latin American literature of the second half of the twentieth century, we should resist the idea that it is a phenomenon occurring exclusively in Latin American authors, or solely in the second half of the twentieth century. These are extra-literary concerns. Rather, we should limit ourselves to classifying themes and devices that are strictly literary in identifying a work of magic realism.

The above has been an attempt to provide a brief summary of the history of the term "magic realism," to distinguish it from some of the literary modes often confused with it, and finally to provide some current opinions on what a definition of magic realism should or might be. In the foregoing discussion, it becomes obvious that no single, precise definition of this literary mode is accepted unanimously. The following essays attempt to illustrate by example --in practical terms and in specific detail-- the manner in which some Latin American authors create their own personal brand of magic realism.

WORKS CITED

Asturias, Miguel Ángel. *Hombres de maíz*. Obras completas. Madrid: Editorial Aguilar, 1969.

Bautista Gutiérrez, Gloria. *Realismo Mágico, cosmos latinoamericano: Teoría y práctica*. Bogotá: América Latina, 1991.

Borges, Jorge Luis. *Discusión*. Buenos Aires: Emecé, 1964.

_____. *Ficciones*. Buenos Aires: Emecé Editores, 1956.

Bravo, José Antonio. *Lo real maravilloso en la narrativa latinoamericana actual*. Lima: Editoriales Unidas, 1978.

Bravo, Víctor. *Magias y maravillas en el continente literario*. Caracas: La Casa de Bello, Colección Zona Tórrida, Letras Universitarias, 1988.

Carpentier, Alejo. *El reino de este mundo*. Mexico City: Editorial Iberoamericana de Publicaciones, 1949.

Flores, Ángel. "Magical Realism in Spanish American Fiction," *Hispania*, 38 (May, 1955).

Chanady, Amaryll Beatrice. *Magical Realism and the Fantastic: Resolved Versus Unresolved Antinomy*. New York & London: Garland Publishing, Inc., 1985.

González Echevarría, Roberto. "Isla a su vuelo fugitiva: Carpentier y el realismo mágico," *Revista Iberoamericana*, 40, #86 (Jan.-March 1974).

Goorden, Anne -B. *Les Origines du "Réalisme Magique dans la littérature Ibéro-Américaine*. Brussels: Recto-Verso, 1981.

Jung, Carl G. *Man and His Symbols*. Garden City, N.Y.: Doubleday & Co., 1964, p. 125.

Leal, Luis. "El realismo mágico en la literatura hispanoamericana," *Cuadernos Americanos*, 4 (1967).

Mena, Lucila-Inés. "Hacia una formulación teórica del realismo mágico," *Bulletin hispanique*, 77, 3-4 (July-December 1975), 395-407.

Menton, Seymour. "Jorge Luis Borges, Magic Realist," *Hispanic Review*, 50, 4 (Autumn 1982), 411-426.

_____. *Magic Realism Rediscovered, 1918-1981*. (July- Dec. 1975), p. 407 Philadelphia: The Art Alliance Press. London & Toronto: Associated University Presses, 1983.

Rodríguez Monegal, Emir. "Realismo mágico versus literatura fantástica: un diálogo de sordos." *Otros mundos otros fuegos*. (Actas del XVI Congreso de Literatura Hispanoameri-

cana). East Lansing, Michigan, August 1973, 25- 37.
Roh, Franz. "El cuento venezolano" in *Letras y Hombres de Venezuela*, 3rd Ed. Madrid: Editorial Mediterráneo, 1974.
Spindler, William. "Magic Realism: A Typology," *Forum for Modern Language Studies*, 39, 1 (1993), 75-85.
Thompson, F.E.J. *Historia y religión de los mayas*. Mexico City: Fondo de Cultura Económica, 1978.
Todorov, Tzvetan. *The Fantastic: A Structural Approach to a Literary Genre*, trans. Richard Howard. Cleveland/London: The Press of Case Western Reserve University, 1973.

Uslar Pietri, Arturo. "De Amadís de Gaula a Miguel Ángel Asturias" in *La busca del nuevo mundo*. Mexico City: Fondo de Cultura Económica, 1969.
_____. "El cuento venezolano" in *Letras y hombres de Venezuela* (1948), 3rd edition Madrid: Editorial Mediterráneo, 1974.
_____ "Realismo mágico" in the newspaper *El Nacional*, Feb. 20, 1985, reprinted in *Godos, insurgentes y visionarios*. Barcelona: Seix Barral, 1986.
Valbuena Briones, Ángel. "Una cala en el realismo mágico," *Cuadernos Americanos*, 166, 5 (Sept.-October 1969), 233-241.
Wheelock, Carter. "Borges, Cortázar, and the Aesthetic of the Vacant Mind," *The International Fiction Review*, 12, 1 (1985), 3-10.
Zlotchew, Clark M. "Entrevista con Antonio Brailovsky," *Alba de América: Revista Literaria*, Vol. 5, Nos. 8 & 9 (1987), 371-383.
_____. *Libido into Literature: The "Primera Época" of Benito Pérez Galdós*, San Bernardino: Borgo Press, 1993, pp. 91-98.
_____. *Voices of the River Plate: Interviews With Writers of Argentina and Uruguay*. San Bernardino: Borgo Press, 1995.

CHAPTER 1
BORGES: MAN AS INSTRUMENT

Some of the adjectives commonly applied to the fiction of Jorge Luis Borges are: detached, cool, cerebral, unemotional. These adjectives accurately reflect the reader's reaction to much of Borges' narrative work. One might attribute this reaction to a supposed absence of conflict in the Argentine author's work, yet this body of literature overflows with conflict, often violent and even lethal. What is missing in a significant proportion of these short stories are elements which could arouse reader identification with the fictional characters.

The struggle between characters in much of Borges' narrative is not perceived as a contest between the forces of good and evil; there is no true hero or even anti-hero. The reader, consequently, feels no attachment for one character over the other, but rather observes the conflict with scientific detachment. The brother of the black man killed by Martin Fierro within the pages of José Hernández' epic poem takes the life of Fierro, the archetypal gaucho, in Borges' "El fin" ("The End"). Curiously, the reader finds it impossible to sympathize either with Fierro, the mythical Argentine hero, or with the avenger who seeks poetic justice. There is no sentiment that either good or evil has been accomplished. Far from being an indication of the author's lack of skill, the reader's reaction to the fictional event is the direct result of Borges' purposeful neutralization of both the Argentine national hero and the universal archetype of the avenger.

The self-important detective of "La muerte y la brújula" ("Death and the Compass") is a pedantic fool whose pedantry is used by the gangster Red Scharlach to trap the detective. He himself betrays no emotion on speaking to the gunman who is about to slay him. He addresses the criminal as though he were speaking to the winner of a friendly game of chess, reviewing his own errors of crime detection in a post mortem of a process that can be conceived of only as a game. In "Los teólogos" ("The Theologians"), God Himself thinks of the two rival churchmen of the early Middle Ages as one person, even though one has had the other burned at the stake for heresy. Even Jesus Christ and Judas Iscariot are partners rather than adversaries in "Tres versiones de Judas" ("Three Versions of Judas").

The struggle, often violent and even deadly, -- between rival knife-fighters, theologians, gauchos, warriors, gangsters and detectives, professors and artists-- is presented with the neutrality of a scientific experiment. The reader witnesses the most savage struggles with the indifference of the bystander who observes a game of chess; the question of good or evil is irrelevant. The reasons for the reader's emotional detachment lies in a world view that underlies Borges' fiction end which can be traced through his poetry and essay as well. Seemingly disparate elements -- essays on Coleridge and on FitzGerald, fiction revolving around gauchos or hoodlums and knife-fights, the tale of a holy man who dreams another man into existence, poetry concerning card games, chess games, rabbinical and kabalistic magic-- are intimately related in their underlying theme, and represent one single, coherent philosophy.

The central idea of Borges' essays, "El enigma de Edward FitzGerald" ("The Enigma of Edward FitzGerald") and "El sueño de Coleridge" (`The Dream of Coleridge"), in which archetypes enter our world through the instrumentation of human beings, is that of man as a tool of higher powers. In the essay on FitzGerald, Borges explores the idea that *The Rubáiyát of Omar Khayyám* is the joint product of a Persian astronomer of the eleventh century and an eccentric English bibliophile of the late nineteenth century. Borges feels that, through "la fortuita conjunción" ("the 'fortuitous conjunction") of these two men, there is produced "un extraordinario poeta, que no se parece a los dos" ("an extraordinary poet, who bears no resemblance to the two [FitzGerald and Omar])" (*Otras Inquisiciones*, 104).

Borges reminds the reader that Omar himself believed in the transmigration of the soul and that the *Rubáiyát* expresses the concept that the history of the universe is a play produced, performed and witnessed by God. This concept, muses Borges, would explain a re-appearance of Omar in the person of FitzGerald, "porque ambos eran, esencialmente, Dios o caras momentáneas de Dios" ("because both were, essentially, God, or momentary faces of God") (Ibid.). Omar and FitzGerald, then, separated by centuries of time and thousands of miles of geography (as well as by culture and language) are instruments in the production of the English poem called *The Rubáiyát of Omar Khayyám*. This concept, which uses historically accurate facts and is logically sound, penetrates beyond the given facts to postulate a kind of magic enveloping them.

The essay "El sueño de Coleridge" dwells on the fact that the English poet Samuel Taylor Coleridge published the poem "Kubla Khan" based on a revelation he experienced in a dream in 1797, without knowing that the subject of that revelation --Kubla Khan's palace at Shang-Tu (Xanadu)-- was itself built in accordance with a plan which the Emperor had also received in a dream.[9] Borges is mystified by the fact that the thirteenth-century Mongol Emperor built a palace according to his vision of its plans in a dream, and that an English poet living five centuries later --and who had no idea that the structure was the product of a dream-- himself dreamed a poem concerning the palace.

Borges feels there must be a purpose behind the two dreams which have resulted in the physical palace and the poem referring to it. Because of the centuries which intervene between the pair of related events, he believes an originator classified as "sobrehumano" ("superhuman") and either "inmortal" ("immortal") or "longevo" ("long-lived") (Ibid. 29) is responsible for them. He then postulates another explanation:

> Acaso un arquetipo no revelado aún a los

> hombres, un objeto eterno (para usar la nomenclatura de Whitehead), esté ingresando paulatinamente en el mundo; su primera manifestación fue el palacio; la segunda el poema. Quien los hubiera comparado habría visto que eran esencialmente iguales (Ibid. 30).

> Perhaps an archetype not yet revealed to men, an eternal object (to use Whitehead's terminology), is gradually entering the world; its first manifestation was the palace; its second was the poem. Anyone comparing them would have seen that they were essentially equal.

The concepts described in the essay on Coleridge are almost identical to those seen in "El enigma de Edward FitzGerald." In both essays, men separated in time and space produce things so closely related that Borges views the men as instruments of a higher intelligence. If Kublai Khan's palace and Coleridge's poem concerning that palace are part of a still unidentified archetype which is gradually entering the world, then Omar Khayyám's Persian poem and Edward FitzGerald's English poem derived from it, by the same line of reasoning, are also part of some archetype. Borges' indication that Omar and FitzGerald are `essentially, God, or momentary faces of God' is analogous to his statement that the Khan and Coleridge are carrying out the designs of a being that is `immortal' or `long-lived.'

In the essay, "La muralla y los libros" ("The Wall and the Books"), Borges feels emotion on contemplating the Chinese Emperor who isolated China in time and space by burning all books written before his reign, and by ordering the construction of the Great Wall. His emotion, unusual in Borges' highly cerebral essays, might possibly stem from a half-realized unconscious association between himself and the Emperor. Both men destroy things created in the past which they feel in some way accuse them, and both men build to enhance their glory. Analogous to Shih Huang Ti's book burning is Borges' behavior in purchasing every copy he can find of his earliest writings in order to burn them (Irby, ix). The construction of the Great Wall keeps the Emperor's name alive for posterity in much the same manner that Borges' later works, collected in his *Obras completas*, are a monument to the Argentine writer.[10]

"Las ruinas circulares" ("The Circular Ruins") is a short story concerning a man who dreams into existence another man, only to find later that he too is the creation of another's dream. The manipulator discovers, to his chagrin, that he is manipulated by a higher intelligence, a higher power. At this point, the reader cannot help but wonder if this series of dreamers and dreamed might be extended even further.

In Borges, the concept of the manipulator manipulated, of human beings as tools of a superior power, is repeated almost obsessively. His poem, "El Golem" ("The Golem"), written in 1958, and part of *El otro, el mismo* (*The Other, the Same*), is based on a Jewish legend which reached Borges via Gustav Meyrink's German novel, *Der Golem*.[11] The poem repeats the theme of "The Circular Ruins," although Borges was not consciously aware of this when he wrote the poem.[12]

In "El Golem," a sixteenth-century rabbi of Prague, by discovering and uttering the secret name of God, animates the previously lifeless form he has molded of clay. After years of attempting to teach his creature to be fully human, the rabbi manages only to teach the Golem to sweep the synagogue floor. The homunculus never learns to speak. The monstrousness of the creature is suggested by Borges: "Algo anormal y tosco hubo en el Golem,/ Ya que a su paso el gato del vecino/ Se escondía" ("There was something abnormal and coarse in the Golem,/ Since the neighbor's cat would hide/ As he passed by") (*Obra poética*, p. 169 and *El otro, el mismo*, 49). The rabbi beholds his handiwork "con ternura/ Y con algún horror" ("with tenderness/ And with a bit of horror") (Ibid.), asking himself why he has engendered this "son" qualified by Borges as "penoso" (a word which literally means 'painful,' but could be translated into English alternately as 'arduous,' 'difficult,' or as 'suffering,' 'afflicted") and why he did not do the wise thing: nothing.

The final stanza of the poem depicts the rabbi in anguish, contemplating his creature. The very last two lines ask the question, "¿Quién nos dirá las cosas que sentía/ Dios, al mirar a su rabino en Praga?" ("Who can tell what God felt, as He looked at his rabbi in Prague?") (*Obra poética*, 170 and *El otro, el mismo*, 49). This is a rhetorical question which, in context, suggests its own answer: just as the rabbi feels tenderness, horror and anguish on looking at the creature he fashioned in his own image, God feels that same tenderness, horror and anguish on contemplating man, and wonders why He made the mistake of creating him. As in "The Circular Ruins" we are faced with a creator who, Borges jolts us into remembering, is himself a creation of a superior being. The poem suggests, as does the short story, that these examples of creators created by other creators might be part of a longer, perhaps infinite, series.

In the same collection of poetry, *El otro, el mismo* ("*The Other, The Same*"), is the poem "Ajedrez" ("Chess") (*Obra poética,* 179-80 and *El otro, el mismo*, 61-62).[13] The first line asserts that the players control the chess pieces. This is what one would expect, although it is obvious, by the end of the poem, that this affirmation is made ironically. The first stanza of the second part of the poem, apparently from the point of view of the chess pieces themselves, gives the impression that the pieces are their own masters. The reader, who knows this is untrue, is congratulated on his perspicacity in the following stanza, which explains that these pieces are deluded because they do not realize that their every move is governed by the adamantine rules of the game and by the will of the players.

The penultimate stanza then deflates the smug reader by declaring that the player himself is just as much a prisoner of that other chess board of "negras noches y de blancos días" ("black nights and white days") (*Obra poética*, 180 and *El otro, el mismo*, 62). Borges, within the poem, credits Omar Khayyám with the idea. The final stanza is explicit in stating that the chess player is moved by God in the same manner in which the chess piece is moved by the player. In paying homage to Omar, Borges is thinking of FitzGerald's lines:

> We are no other than a moving row
> Of Magic Shadow-shapes that come and go
> Round with the Sun-illumined Lantern held
> In Midnight by the Master of the Show;
>
> But helpless Pieces of the Game He plays
> Upon this Chequer-board of Nights and Days;
> Hither and thither moves, and checks, and slays,
> And one by one back in the Closet lays.
> (*Rubáiyát*, 145-146).[14]

When Borges writes, in the last stanza of "Ajedrez" ("Chess"), "Dios mueve al jugador, y éste, la pieza" ("God moves the player, and the player moves the piece"), the reader cannot help but mentally extend the metaphor, and wonder whether there are other gods behind God. Borges immediately supports this conjecture by adding, "¿Qué dios detrás de Dios la trama empieza/ De polvo y tiempo y sueño y agonías?" ("What god behind God begins the weaving of this weft of dust and time and dream and agony?") (*Obra poética*, 180 and *El otro, el mismo*, 62)). Borges goes beyond the limits set by Omar and FitzGerald, suggesting an infinite series of chess player/gods.

The thrust of "Chess" is to expose human beings as pawns manipulated by forces more powerful than they. This concept, borrowed from FitzGereld's English adaptation of Omar Khayyám's poetry, is also illustrated in Borges' essay on FitzGerald and Omar, and is the central theme of Borges' poem, "The Golem" as well as of his essay "The Dream of Coleridge," and his short story, "The Circular Ruins." The same theme underlies Borges' poem, "El truco," a poem included in *Fervor de Buenos Aires*, ostensibly about the card game called truco.

The forty cards of truco are manipulated by the players, but these players necessarily repeat the moves of former players who have died, "hecho que inmortaliza un poco,/ apenas,/ a los compañeros muertos que callan" ("a fact which immortalizes somewhat,/ scarcely,/ their dead companions who remain silent") (*Obra poética,* 28). The kings, queens, and jacks depicted on the cards are characters, like the kings, queens and other pieces in chess, apparently manipulated by their gods, the players.

Borges writes, "En los lindes de la mesa/ el vivir común se detiene./ Adentro hay otro país" ("Within the confines of the [card] table/ ordinary life comes to a halt,/ Inside there is another country") (Ibid. 27). It is as though the players, looming above this country, this world of the card game, controlled the fate of the puny creatures who come to life within that world, although those creatures -- arrogant kings, queens and jacks among them-- do not suspect this. Yet the players, holding the cards and thinking themselves in control, are unaware that the game of truco is a ritual in which they --mortal, interchangeable, replaceable human beings-- are the priests who tend the timeless altar just as their deceased brethren did before them. Reading this early poem, from *Fervor de Buenos Aires* (*Enthusiasm for Buenos Aires*) (1923), with hindsight, with the insight gained by reading Borges' later writings, one senses that "El truco" anticipates "Ajedrez" ("Chess"). The card players, like their fellows the chess players, believe they are the manipulators, but are nothing more than ephemeral instruments of the immortal game itself.[15]

Knives, in the works of Borges, have a life of their own, and exert power over men. In "El encuentro" ("The Encounter"), one man accuses another of cheating at cards, and challenges him to fight. Someone mentions the collection of daggers in the house, and opens the showcase that contains them. Each man chooses a dagger and goes outdoors to fight. The challenger kills the other, but immediately bends over the body, sobbing uncontrollably, to beg forgiveness.

Everyone present is sure the two men know nothing about dueling with knives, yet they surprisingly fight with great skill. These anomalies are explained when, years later, the narrator finds that the daggers used in the duel had belonged to two men who hated each other and continually attempted to search each other out in order to engage in combat. This encounter never took place because they died before having had the opportunity to fight each other.

The narrator concludes that the slaying he had witnessed was actually the end of the long-sought confrontation between the old enemies, or rather, between their weapons:

> Maneco Uriarte no mató a Duncan; las armas, no los hombres, pelearon. Habían dormido, lado a lado, en una vitrina, hasta que las manos las despertaron. Acaso se agitaron al despertar; por eso tembló el puño de Uriarte, por eso tembló el puño de Duncan. Las dos sabían pelear--no sus instrumentos, los hombres--y pelearon bien esa noche (*El informe de Brodie*, p. 60).

> Maneco Uriarte did not kill Duncan; the weapons, not the men, fought. They had slept, side by side, in a glass case, until they were awakened by those hands. Perhaps they quivered when they awoke; that is why Uriarte's hand trembled, that is why Duncan's hand trembled. The two [weapons] knew how to fight --not their instruments, the men-- and they fought well that night.

The foregoing explains why two men who know nothing of knife fighting appear to know a great deal: it is the daggers, not the men, that are skilled. The knives use the men as instruments of their skill rather than vice versa. This also explains why Uriarte suffers from overpowering remorse once he kills Duncan: it was not his own will that slew the other man; it was that of his dagger. The events narrated --the fight itself, the death, the remorse-- are all within the realm of the possible, and are described in a realistic way. Yet the narrator sees certain anomalies in the situation which he explains, in a matter-of-fact manner, as having what the average reader would consider a supernatural cause. The realism is magical.

The narrator concludes, "Las cosas duran más que la gente" ("Things last longer than people") (Ibid. p. 61), and wonders if the story has really ended or if the two daggers will meet yet again in the future. This suggests a possibly infinite series of deadly clashes in which men will be the instruments of the knives. It is not only the concept of man as the instrument of objects he believes he controls (chess pieces, cards, knives) which links the story "The Encounter" with the poetry concerning chess and the card game of truco, but also the idea that human beings are short lived (an indisputable fact) while the activities in which they engage are eternal.

In "The Encounter" the narrator's comment that "Las cosas duran más que la gente." ("Things last longer than people") is remarkably similar in concept to the assertion, "Cuando los jugadores se hayan ido./Cuando el tiempo los haya consumido./Ciertamente no habrá cesado el rito./.../Como el otro, este juego es infinito" ("When the players have gone their ways,/When time has consumed them,/Surely the rite will not have ceased./.../Like the other one, this game is infinite." in the poem "Ajedrez" ("Chess") (*Obra poética*, p. 179). And in "El truco," Borges succinctly remarks, "los jugadores en fervor presente /copian remotas bazas" ("the players in their present enthusiasm/copy far-removed tricks") (Ibid. p. 28). In other words, although the card players are enthusiastically playing their hands at the present moment, and, no doubt, believe they are being original in their handling of the game, they are actually repeating the behavior of card players of long ago and far away.

Human beings are tools of some higher power in

many of the essays, short stories and poems of Borges. We have seen them as instruments of inanimate objects, such as knives, in the short story "The Encounter," and of the eternal ritual of the game of chess in the poem "Chess." Daggers and a chess game may seem to be very different entities, yet both involve a form of highly skilled combat. Furthermore, a statement in "The Encounter" explicitly links the knife fight to the game of chess: "Yo había previsto la pelea como un caos de acero, pero pude seguirla, o casi seguirla, como si fuera un ajedrez" ("I had foreseen the fight as a chaos of steel, but I was able to follow it, or almost follow it, as though it were a game of chess") (*Obra poética*, 56-57).

In the short story, "Juan Muraña" (*Informe de Brodie*, 65-72), a feeble old widow thinks of her late husband's dagger as being her husband himself, and uses the knife to murder the landlord who is going to evict her. She tells the narrator that her (deceased) husband, a notorious knife-fighter, killed the landlord. If this frail old woman can kill as efficiently as her late husband, a man skilled in the use of cold steel, the thought occurs that it was the dagger itself which employed both husband and wife to satisfy its own thirst for blood.

Juan Dahlmann, in "El Sur" ("The South"), finds himself obliged to fight and probably die because he is handed a knife. The weapon is tossed to him, not by a man of flesh and blood, but by an old gaucho who was "como fuera del tiempo, en una eternidad" ("sort of outside of time, in an eternity") (*Ficciones*, 193), and in whom Dahlmann saw "una cifra del Sur (del Sur que era suyo)" ("a compendium of the South [of the South that was his]"), (Ibid. 195).

The old gaucho is an idea, a symbol of a way of life which has disappeared but for which Dahlmann yearns. When the gaucho tosses the knife to the protagonist, "Era como si el Sur hubiera resuelto que Dahlmann aceptara el duelo" ("It was as though the South had decided that Dahlmann should accept the challenge") (Ibid). The South, for Dahlmann, is what the Old West is for North Americans:

a mythical time and place in which a man lived more in harmony with nature and did not depend on an overly complex society for survival, where a man's personal valor was the highest virtue, and where a man was free. The Argentine gaucho and his dagger have symbolic values equivalent to those of the American cowboy and his six-shooter.

Dahlmann prefers to die fighting, a knife in his hand, under the open skies of the Pampa, rather than to expire passively, defenselessly, within the walls of a Buenos Aires hospital. For him, the knife represents freedom. However, Dahlmann's sense of freedom is as illusory as that of the chess pieces and the chess players, of the kings, queens and jacks of the game of truco and the card players, of Uriarte and Duncan in their duel. The old gaucho's dagger forces Dahlmann to fight and probably die: "Era como si el Sur hubiera resuelto que Dahlmann aceptara el duelo" ("It was as though the South had decided that Dahlmann should accept the challenge"). The dagger, proceeding from the gaucho who represents a way of life referred to as "The South," uses Dahlmann as an instrument for keeping that way of life alive.

In "Ton, Uqbar, Orbis Tertius," human beings create a fictitious country and then an entire planet by means of spurious encyclopedic articles, essays and reports. Yet if in the end "El mundo será Tlon" ("The world will be Tlon") (*Ficciones*, 34), because the languages and sciences of Tlon are being taught in school, along with the history of that planet, then the world called Tlon is an archetype which employs men as its instruments for entering our world, for supplanting our world.

Borges' short story "Emma Zunz is problematic. While planning to murder Loewenthal --because he ruined her father's reputation, thereby indirectly causing his death by suicide-- Emma dreams she is aiding "la Justicia de Dios" ("God's Justice") to vanquish "la justicia humana" ("human justice") (*El Aleph*, 64). She wishes to avoid punishment, the narrator tells us, not because she fears it, but because of her capacity as "un instrumento de la Justicia" ("an instrument of Justice") (Ibid.). The foreign sailor whom Emma permits to take her virginity --in order for her to be able to provide physical "evidence" that Loewenthal raped her-- is, for Emma, a mere tool: "El hombre... fue una herramienta para Emma como ésta lo fue para él, pero ella sirvió para el goce y él para la justicia" ("The man... was a tool for Emma as she was for him, but she served as an instrument of pleasure and he as an instrument of justice" (Ibid. 63).

The story is different from the writings we have been examining, because Emma believes she is the agent of a higher power, only to find later that she acted on her own. When she finally confronts Loewenthal, "más que la urgencia de vengar a su padre, Emma sintió la de castigar el ultraje padecido por ello. No podía no matarlo, después de esa minuciosa deshonra" ("Emma felt, rather than the urgent need to avenge her father, that of punishing [someone for] the outrage she had suffered on account of it [the entire situation]. She could not not kill him, after that meticulous dishonor") (My emphasis, Ibid. 64). Still, it is not unreasonable to affirm that Emma really is the tool of a higher power; otherwise she would not have debased herself in the first place. Furthermore, if one can not not do something, then one is in the power of an external force.

The entire story resembles a chess game. Loewenthal embezzles funds from the firm, and rises in position from manager to proprietor, while Emma's father, falsely accused by Loewenthal, is forced to flee the country and finally commit suicide: Emma's father is "rooked" and removed from the chess board. By means of an intricate strategy involving another piece's capture (the sailor), Emma, the white queen, checkmates the opposing king.[16] Emma Zunz, the instrument of God's Justice (with a capital J), is a valuable piece in the hand of God, Whose adversary is "human justice" in lower case letters.

The highly varied array of characters and situations —both fictional and real-- encountered in the pages of Borges' writings in three genres, cloaks one continually reiterated theme. The world view which underlies the essays of *Otras inquisiciones*, the poetry of *Fervor de Buenos Aires* and *El otro, el mismo*, as well as the short stories of *Ficciones, El Aleph*, and *El informe de Brodie*, runs counter to the concept of free will. The idea of man, the great manipulator, as a mere pawn in the hands of God, as Omar Khayyám would have it, or even a series of gods, as Borges suggests, leaves no place for concepts of right and wrong, of innocence and guilt.

If human beings are no more than instruments, they cannot be either praised or condemned. It is this determinism in Borges' *Weltanschauung*, explicit in his essay and poetry, implicit in his fiction,, which forestalls reader identification with Borges' characters and results in a detached, cerebral reading of his fiction. The reader sympathizes with or feels antipathy toward the characters in the narratives of Jorge Luis Borges no more than he/she would sympathize with or feel antipathy toward two strangers playing a game of chess, or toward marionettes manipulated by other marionettes, manipulated by still other marionettes, ad infinitum.

WORKS CONSULTED

Borges, Jorge Luis. *El Aleph*. Buenos Aires: Emecé, 1961.
_____. *Ficciones*. Buenos Aires: Emecé, 1956.
_____. *El informe de Brodie*. Buenos Aires: Emecé, 1960.
_____. *El otro, el mismo*. Buenos Aires: Emecé, 1969.
_____. *Obra poética*. Buenos Aires: Emecé, 1964.
_____. *Other Inquisitions 1937-1952*. Trans. Ruth L.C. Simms. Austin: University of Texas Press, 1964.
_____. *Otras inquisiciones*. Buenos Aires: Emecé, 1960.
Denevi, Marco. *Ceremonia secreta y otros cuentos de Marco Denevi*. Ed. Donald A. Yates. New York: MacMillan, 1965.
FitzGerald, Edward. *The Rubáiyát of Omar Khayyám*. Roslyn, N.Y.: Walter J. Black, 1942.
Irby, James. Introduction. Jorge Luis Borges, *Other Inquisitions 1937-1952*. Trans. Ruth L.C. Simms. Austin: University of Texas Press, 1964.
Jung, C[arl] G. *The Archetypes and the Collective Unconscious*. Trans R.F.C. Hull. Second ed. Bollingen Series XX. Princeton: Princeton University Press, 1968.
Pickenhayn, Jorge Oscar. *Borges a través de sus libros*. Buenos Aires: Plus Ultra, 1979.
Sorrentino, Fernando. *Siete conversaciones con Jorge Luis Borges*. Buenos Aires: Casa Pardo, 1973.
_____. *Seven Conversations with Jorge Luis Borges*. Translation, additional notes, appendix of personalities mentioned by Borges, and translator's foreword by Clark M. Zlotchew. Troy, N.Y.: Whitston, 1982.
Zlotchew, Clark M. "Entrevista con Jorge Luis Borges," *Hispania*, 69, 1 (March 1986), 151-53.
_____. "Tlon, Llhuros, N. Daly, J>L> Borges," *Modern Fiction Studies*, 19, 3 (Autumn 1973), 453-59.
_____. *Voices of the River Plate: Interviews with Writers of Argentina and Uruguay*. San Bernardino (CA): Borgo, 1995.

CHAPTER 2
BORGES: MAGIC REALISM IN REAL LIFE

Jorge Luis Borges' pantheistic preoccupation with the concept that all authors are one author, although they may live in various eras and locations and are known by different names, is too well known to be insisted upon. The fact that Borges himself may have been an example of these concepts in real life is another matter; Borges himself had no idea that this might have been the case.

These concepts are but one facet of a more general idea entertained by Borges: a supreme and eternal Mind conceives thoughts in the abstract and then translates them into the world as we know it through the instrumentality of human beings. Before moving on to suggest how Borges -- along with the first Emperor of China and a twentieth-century artist of Ithaca, New York-- may have been one of a series of human instruments of the eternal Mind, Borges' ideas along these lines should be examined. Of the many possible examples of Borges' work which illustrate this blend of Platonism and Pantheism, two will suffice for the purpose of this brief study: "El enigma de Edward FitzGerald" ("The Enigma of Edward FitzGerald") and "El sueño de Coleridge" ("Coleridge's Dream") in his collection of essays, *Otras inquisiciones.*

In the essay on FitzGerald, the point is made that through some "fortuitous conjunction of a Persian astronomer [Omar Khayyam] who condescended to [engage in] poetry, of an eccentric Englishman who makes his way through Oriental and Hispanic books [Edward FitzGerald], perchance without completely understanding them, there results an extraordinary poet who resembles neither of the two" (*Otras...*, 104).[17] Borges comments on the belief held by some critics that FitzGerald's *Rubáiyát* is truly an English poem with Persian points of reference. He adds: "FitzGerald interpoló, afinó e inventó, pero sus *Rubaiyat* parecen exigir de nosotros que las leamos como persas y antiguas" (Ibid. 104). ("FitzGerald interpolated, refined and invented, but his Rubáiyát seem to require that we read them as Persian and ancient").

Borges reminds us that Omar himself professed the doctrine (which is both Platonic and Pythagorean) that the soul may lodge in several different bodies at various points in time, and that the *Rubáiyát* are highly pantheistic in expressing the idea that the history of the universe is a spectacle conceived, represented, and contemplated by God. Borges muses that the latter concept would allow for a recreation of the Persian by the Englishman, "Porque ambos eran, esencialmente, Dios o caras momentáneas de Dios" ("since both were, essentially, God or momentary faces of God") (Ibid. 104).

Borges ends the essay reflecting on the mystery of all forms of collaboration, assuming that this particular case is more mysterious than others because the two men were so completely different one from the other that they probably would not have become friends had they known each other in life (Ibid. 105); therefore, death as well as vicissitudes and the passage of time actually served the purpose of merging the two men into one single poet. This essay, then, is highly representative of a theme repeatedly insisted on in the work of the Argentinean writer.

The essay "El sueño de Coleridge" concentrates on the fact that in 1816 the English poet Samuel Taylor Coleridge published "Kubla Khan" based on the unfinished poem which had come to him as a revelation --in a series of visual images as well as their verbal counterpart-- in a dream he experienced in 1797. Borges goes on to mention that it was not until twenty years after the publication of "Kubla Khan" that the first western translation of a universal history (the *Compendium of History* by Rashid ed-Din, dating from the fourteenth century) appeared in Paris with the information that Kublai Khan's palace at Shang-Tu (Xanadu) was built in accordance with a plan which the

Emperor had seen in a dream.

There is absolutely no evidence of any text which Coleridge could have read before the publication of his own work with the information that the palace itself was built in accordance with the inspiration of a dream. Accordingly, it is not the mere fact that Coleridge "received" his poem in a dream only after reading a passage describing the construction of the palace at Xanadu that fascinates and mystifies Borges; it is the fact that in the thirteenth century the Mongol Emperor of China built a palace according to his vision of it in a dream, and that an English poet living five centuries later, who had no idea that the edifice was the result of a dream, himself dreamed a poem concerning that structure.

"El primer sueño agregó a la realidad un palacio; el segundo, que se produjo cinco siglos después, un poema (o principio de poema) sugerido por el palacio..." ("The first dream added a palace to reality; the second, produced five centuries later, a poem (or the beginning of a poem) suggested by the palace...") (Ibid. 29). Borges believes that there is some sort of definite plan operating on the production of two dreams of such great similarity and that, based on the huge length of time intervening between the two dreams, a superhuman originator ("ejecutor sobrehumano") is indicated (Ibid.).

The Argentinean author comments on the futility of attempting to ascertain the purpose motivating the Being he describes as "inmortal" ("immortal") or "longevo" ("long-lived"), but declares that this purpose probably has not been attained as yet. It was confirmed in 1691 that all that was left of the Khan's palace were ruins. It is a fact that only fifty lines of the three hundred-verse poem dreamed by Coleridge have been set down on paper. Borges draws the conclusion that the series of visions and the works resulting from them have not ended. He muses: "Quizá la serie de los sueños no tenga fin, quizá la clave esté en el último" ("Perhaps the series of dreams has no end; perhaps the key is found in the last [dream]") (p. 29).

Borges then postulates another explanation: "Possibly an archetype not yet revealed to men, an eternal object (to use Whitehead's terminology), is gradually entering the world; its first manifestation was the palace; its second was the poem. Anyone comparing them would have seen that they were essentially equal" (p. 30). In this essay on Coleridge's dream, we are presented once more with two men who create basically the same entity, or rather, two facets of that entity. Furthermore, these two men, separated in time and space, are seen to be the instruments of either a divine intelligence or of an archetype which employs individuals for the purpose of transferring this ideal into the real world.

Ironically, Borges himself is involved --without realizing it-- in the processes he describes in both "El enigma de Edward FitzGerald" and "El sueño de Coleridge." These two essays form part of Borges' book of philosophical essays titled *Otras inquisiciones* (*Other Inquisitions* or *Other Inquiries*), first published in 1952. That Borges himself may be one of a series of men, separated one from the other in time and space, who have unwittingly cooperated to bring some archetype into our world, will become clearer after we deal with another essay, the first one in *Otras inquisiciones:* "La muralla y los libros" ("The Wall and the Books").

In "The Wall and the Books" Borges ponders the possible motivation for as well as the philosophical implications of the actions of Shih Huang Ti, "primer Emperador" ("first Emperor") of China", who performed two prodigious feats: he ordered the construction of the Great Wall and the burning of all books written before he was Emperor. Shih Huang Ti, referred to as the "first" Emperor (his destruction of history erased any records of previous emperors), attempted to isolate China in space (by the Wall) and in time (by the destruction of the past).

It is essential to note that the series of essays here referred to is entitled *Otras inquisiciones* (*Other Inquisitions*), yet one will not be able to find in the complete works of Jorge Luis Borges a prior collection called simply *Inquisiciones* (*Inquisitions* or *Inquiries*), as would be logical. This gives rise to some important questions: Why are there "other" inquiries if there were no earlier inquiries? What is the meaning of the word "other" in the title?

The truth is that Borges' very first volume of essays bore the title *Inquisiciones* (1925). However, later considering those original *Inquisiciones* to be nothing more than exercises in avant-garde writing which were both dogmatic and affected, Borges refused to allow them to be included in his *Obras completas* (*Complete Works*). Furthermore, he not only refused to permit reprinting of that book but actively sought out all copies of them in order to buy them from the owners for the purpose of destroying them.[18]

Perhaps the similarity of behavior observed in the destruction of books by the Emperor and by Borges is somewhat more than superficial. In the first paragraph of "The Wall and the Books" Borges states his motives for pondering this case. The fact that those two formidable projects (construction of an immense wall against the barbarians and the abolition of the past) "procedieran de una persona y fueran de algún modo sus atributos, inexplicablemente me satisfizo y, a la vez, me inquietó" ("were initiated by one person and in some way were attributes of that person, inexplicably satisfied me and, at the same time, disturbed me") (Ibid. p. 9). "Indagar las razones de esa emoción es el fin de esta nota" ("To delve into the reasons for that emotion is the goal of this note") (Ibid.).

In trying to comprehend the conflicting emotions of satisfaction and disturbance engendered in him by the facts mentioned, he wanders through a maze of philosophical thought as well as historical and esthetical discussion. Why would the usually cerebral, unemotional Borges uncharacteristically experience strong emotions in contemplating Shih Huang Ti? Perhaps it is because Borges sensed, on some level, that he, Borges, and the Emperor are more closely linked than might appear.

Some of Borges' conjectures on the Chinese Emperor's motivation for destroying history could apply equally well to Borges' motives for erasing the memory of his *Inquisiciones*. Shih Huang Ti, Borges muses, might have wished to obliterate the canonical books because they were his accusers.[19] Shih Huang Ti, "tal vez, quiso abolir todo el pasado para abolir un solo recuerdo: la infamia de su madre" ("perhaps, wished to abolish the entire past in order to abolish one single memory: his mother's infamy") (Ibid. p. 10).

After much weighing possibilities, Borges sees as the result of one of these possibilities, the image of "un rey desengañado que destruyó lo que antes defendía" ("a disillusioned king who destroyed what he once used to defend") (Ibid. p. 11). As the monarch destroyed records of the past to enhance the value of his more recent accomplishments, so does Borges. As the Emperor caused the disappearance of books and in doing so destroyed, in his disillusionment, what he used to defend, Borges destroyed books which contain a style of writing which he used to defend and with which he was later disenchanted; the books happen to be copies of *Inquisiciones*, the collection of essays mentioned above which he wrote and later regretted.

The emperor built as he destroyed, and for one single purpose: the augmentation of his glory. Borges has created, too: the work he produced since the first collection of essays. This work, without any doubt, has made him justly renowned. One may wonder, then, at the conflicting emotions (satisfaction and disturbance) uncharacteristically produced --and mentioned in writing by the author. This admission, among the notoriously clinical, unemotional writings of Borges, elicited by supposedly philosophical ruminations, no less, is anomalous. It is inexplicable to Borges himself. One may wonder, then, if Borges subconsciously sensed he was in some mysterious way intimately associated with Shih Huang Ti in the introduction of an archetype (as yet undefined) into the real world.

If we permit our imaginations to accept as possible Borges' ideas on a series of human beings, separated in time and space, but who are essentially the same person, yet a third man is involved with Shih Huang Ti and Jorge Luis Borges. In fact, we can see Borges' connection with this third person, Norman Daly, in a manner much more obvious and startling than Borges' association with the ancient Chinese emperor, even though Borges never met or even heard of Daly.[20] What's more, Daly, while having heard of Borges, was not acquainted with his work.[21]

Before proceeding to discuss Daly's work, however, it is necessary to consider one more work of Borges, a work of fiction this time. "Tlon, Uqbar, Orbis Tertius," in *Ficciones*, is a thought-provoking tale of the fantastic presented in the form of notes dealing with non-existent books. Briefly stated, Borges claims he finds references to a country (Uqbar) in an obscure encyclopedia. He has never heard of such a country and can neither accurately locate its geographic position nor find mention of it in any other set of the same encyclopedia. Similarly, no indication of the minutely described Uqbar is to be found in other reference books either.

Some years later he happens upon what appears to be one volume of an extensive encyclopedia dealing with an otherwise unknown planet. Borges provides a summary of the architecture, philosophy, linguistic features, geography, mythology, history, literature, and other features of the arts and sciences of the planet. These features, in addition to being highly imaginative while at the same time plausible -- and, therefore, intellectually disconcerting-- possess the advantage of being highly ordered and logical. Furthermore, while unquestionably exotic, indeed alien to our experience, this planet's literary concepts and philosophy are presented in a manner which appeals to our esthetic sensibilities.

Borges finally informs us of the origin of the singular encyclopedias: a secret benevolent society in Europe at the beginning of the seventeenth century, whose members included individuals learned in various fields, decided to invent a country. Later, realizing that one generation would not be equal to a task of such magnitude, each of the masters would choose a disciple to continue the task. In the nineteenth century the organization turns up in the United States, where a millionaire decides the project of inventing a country is too modest and convinces the others to expand the task to that of fabricating an entire planet. Briefly, then, this is the explanation for the appearance of the books and encyclopedias about a non-existent country and on an equally non-existent planet in such convincing style.

At this point, readers cannot help but question everything they think they know. The process described above is so absolutely feasible (though implausible), that it poses an epistemological problem. A determined secret society with sufficient resources at its disposal, bent on convincing the world of the existence of an apocryphal country or even planet, could conceivably do just that. The overwhelming bulk of our knowledge of this complex universe comes to us, not from direct observation, but from reading or hearing what others claim to be true. How do I know there really are entities called atoms or viruses if I can't see them? How do I know there is a place called Wyoming or China if I've never been there? Not from personal experience, but from what might be labeled hearsay.

How do I know that Wyoming or China are not fictional entities invented by a well-endowed secret society, using Hollywood-style techniques, whether operating for profit, or from sinister motives or just for fun and games, the way Borges' fictional society does? CNN and all the rest of the media tell us there is a war in Chechnya, we believe it, whether that country actually exists or not. The fact that the activities described in Borges' short story could actually take place --there is nothing supernatural about them up to this point-- is disconcerting.

The Protocols of the Elders of Zion is an infamous forgery created in Czarist Russia which purports to prove that world Jewry is engaged in a plot to control the entire world. This preposterous hoax was widely circulated in Europe during the late nineteenth century and has recently appeared around the world from England to Japan and is being enthusiastically disseminated in Moslem nations. Millions of people firmly believe that this forged document represents the absolute truth.

The *History* of Herodotus makes claims we now know to have been impossible, yet they are stated as fact and were believed by Europeans for centuries. There is nothing incredible, then, about the main premise of "Tlon." But Borges takes matters even further.

The labor of the secret society in "Tlon, Uqbar, Orbis Tertius" reaches the point at which three-dimensional objects begin to appear mysteriously, at times engraved with letters corresponding to one of the alphabets of Tlon. The number of these strange objects increases as time passes. The increase in the appearance of artifacts from the non-existent planet is accompanied by the printing of manuals, anthologies, translations, and reprints dealing with various features of that planet. Under the pressure of all this evidence, "[C]asi inmediatamente, la realidad cedió en más de un punto. Lo cierto es que anhelaba ceder." ("[A]lmost immediately, reality began to yield in more than one point. The truth is that it longed to yield") (*Ficciones*, p. 33). The reason for this predisposition of the truth to give way to fiction is that in recent years:

> Hace diez años bastaba cualquier simetría con apariencia de orden --el materialismo dialéctico, el antisemitismo, el nazismo-- para embelesar a los hombres. ¿Cómo no someterse a Tlon, a la minuciosa y vasta evidencia de un planeta ordenado? Inútil responder que la realidad también está ordenada. Quizá lo esté, pero de acuerdo a leyes divinas --traduzco: a leyes inhumanas-- que no acabamos nunca de percibir. Tlon será un laberinto, pero es un laberinto urdido por hombres, un laberinto destinado a que lo descifren los hombres. (*Ficciones*, 33-34.)

> Ten years ago any kind of symmetry with the appearance of order --dialectical materialism, anti-Semitism, Nazism-- has been sufficient to fascinate mankind. How could one not submit to Tlon, to the detailed vast body of evidence of an orderly planet?

It is useless to respond that Reality is orderly too. Perhaps it is, but in accordance with <u>divine</u> laws --I translate: with <u>non-human</u> laws-- which we never quite manage to perceive. Tlon may well be a labyrinth, but it is a labyrinth planned by men, a labyrinth destined to be deciphered by men. (My emphasis).

In other words, humankind, yearning to live in a world it is capable of understanding, prefers the man-made world (a fictional world) to the real world. This is an explanation, of course, for the reason that people love fiction. But in Borges' story, the fiction of Tlon is presented so strongly and so multifacetically that suspension of disbelief is absolute; the fiction is finally accepted as the truth permanently.

The languages, the harmonious history, pharmacology, and several other sciences of Tlon are already being taught in the schools, we are told. In fact, the history of Tlon being disseminated by the Department of Education has wiped out the history which Borges was taught in his youth. "...ya en las memorias un pasado ficticio ocupa el sitio de otro..." ("...a fictitious past takes the place of another past in people's memory...") (*Ficciones*, p. 34).

This situation, perhaps not so coincidentally, is reminiscent of the outcome desired by the "first" Emperor of China, Shih Huang Ti, as well as of results obtained by modern totalitarian states in which people are not only physically annihilated, but all records and references to them are obliterated as well, so that they might as well never have existed. In "Tlon, Uqbar, Orbis Tertius," the world has been completely changed by a group of individuals, and the efforts continue. Borges foresees the disappearance from the Earth of the Spanish language, of French, of English... "El mundo será Tlon" ("The world will be Tlon") (*Ficciones*, p. 34).

Unknown to Borges, some of the first steps in a process eerily similar to that described in "Tlon, Uqbar, Orbis Tertius" have already been taken in the real world. Furthermore, the process has been initiated by a man who has not read the story concerning Tlon. In February of 1972, the Andrew Dickson White Museum of Art (Cornell University) in Ithaca, New York, presented what appeared to be an archeological display dealing with the "lost" civilization of Llhuros. Included in "The Civilization of Llhuros" were exotic artifacts of wood, ceramic, and metal. These urns, religious objects and weapons could be found affixed to walls or in glass cases and appeared to be quite ancient, judging from the corrosion in evidence. Labels informed the visitor that the "fragment of a mural" was unearthed at Houndee or that the trallib (Llhuroscian for "vessel for holding oil") was unearthed at a dig in Vanibo. The exposition contained over one hundred items, including a map of the excavated area and a menstrual chart.

Needless to say, or perhaps not so needless, the display was a good-humored hoax deriding archeological exhibits. This ingenious bit of craftsmanship was created painstakingly during the five years preceding the exhibition by Norman Daly, an artist who invented an entire civilization, presenting the public with "relics" of that culture. The "remains" of Llhuroscian society were manufactured for the most part out of the debris of our twentieth-century industrialized and commercialized society (detergent bottles, styrofoam, packing boxes, retouched photographs, etc.) transformed by Daly's ingenuity and deftness with the use of acrylic paints (for "corroding" surfaces).

The exhibit was not limited to artifacts; Daly composed highly evocative music, which was executed electronically on the Moog synthesizer, and had it piped in, thereby setting a mood which might be thought of as otherworldly. There was even a "scholarly" catalogue filled with examples of the amorous poetry of Llhuros.

Although "The Civilization of Llhuros" is a burlesque, its creator sees in it another dimension: "On one level, the show is meant to appeal to people's need to suspend reality, to their nostalgia for things they've never experienced. And by using objects of modern civilization, I've tried to get people to rediscover the beauty of our own industrial designs" (Michener, 93).

The rationale expressed here is startlingly similar to that expressed by Borges for the truth's predisposition to yield to man-made Tlon. Daly adds: "I really don't think Llhuros is fictitious at all" (Michener, 93). The reality of Llhuros may have imposed itself on many of the visitors to the exhibit, which would affect the populations of the many cities in which the show was presented.[22] At the showing in Rochester (N.Y.), I myself heard comments by at least three persons indicating their belief in the authenticity of Llhuros, while admitting their previous ignorance of that civilization.

From the foregoing, it is not inadmissible to glimpse, in the "real" world, the involvement, *unknown to Borges*, of Borges himself with the concepts he entertains in his writings, be they fiction or essay (and it is difficult to draw a distinct dividing line between those two genres in his work).

The essays, "El enigma de Edward FitzGerald" and "El sueño de Coleridge " operating along lines showing affinities with both Plato and Spinoza, present the idea that all poets are but one poet and that eternal objects or archetypes, the products of an Infinite Mind, force their way into the "real" world by the instrumentality of human beings.[23] These, although seemingly distinct individuals, are linked as are the various instruments of an orchestra in producing (or receiving and reproducing) a symphony.

The essay "La muralla y los libros" ("The Wall and the Books") is the first tenuous indication that Borges may be involved in the phenomena he contemplates. However, it is when one becomes aware of Norman Daly's exhibit, Llhuros, while considering the fictional "Tlon, Uqbar, Orbis Tertius" in which an "archetype" (in the tradition of Kublai Khan's palace) gradually enters the world to the extent that the world becomes that archetype, that this involvement of Borges becomes impossible to overlook.

In addition, if we accept the possibility of the concepts discussed in the essays dealing with FitzGerald-Omar Khayyam and with Coleridge-Kublai Khan, we might be tempted (keeping in mind that Borges never knew of Norman Daly and that Daly had not read "Tlon") to conceive of the Emperor Shih Huang Ti, the poet Jorge Luis Borges, and the artist Norman Daly as being facets of one being or several instruments of one idea in the process of entering the world. The identity of that idea is not yet known, but in achieving its end it destroys the past while constructing something new.

The Chinese Emperor destroyed the past while building the Great Wall. Borges destroyed his first book of essays, *Inquisiciones*, while writing his later work. Daly destroyed detergent containers, packing boxes and other products of our modern civilization in order to create "trallibs" and bronze doors, thereby imposing Llhuros upon Earth just as Borges' Tlon replaces Earth. Norman Daly has stated that he does not believe Llhuros to be fictional at all; some observers of the exhibit share that feeling.

In an interview, Borges once told me, "I myself don't know who I am." I suggested, "You are the instrument of an archetype that is trying to enter the material world, aren't you?" He answered, "Well, yes. That's a good explanation." (*Voices*, 39). He may very well be that instrument, along with Shih Huang Ti and Norman Daly.

WORKS CONSULTED

Borges, Jorge Luis. *Ficciones*. Buenos Aires: Emecé, 1956.
_____. *Other Inquisitions 1937-1952*. Austin: University of Texas Press, 1964.
_____. *Otras inquisiciones*. Buenos Aires: Emecé, 1960.
Daly, Norman. Letter to C.M. Zlotchew of June 21, 1973.
Michener, Charles. "The Fabulous Llhuroscians," *Newsweek*, Feb. 28, 1972.
Zlotchew, Clark M. *Voices of the River Plate: Interviews with Writers of Argentina and Uruguay* (San Bernardino: Borgo Press, 1995.

CHAPTER 3

BORGES AND THE FRENCH "NEW NOVEL":

FICTION WRAPPED IN FICTION

Almost a half century ago, Borges enumerated four procedures found in the literature of fantasy from the earliest times.[24] These procedures, which permit the writer effectively to destroy reality, are: (1) the literary work within the literary work; (2) the contamination of reality with dream; (3) the voyage in time; (4) the double. Carter Wheelock perceptively notes that the double "dissolves human personality and makes it subordinate to archetypal actions and forms," while the voyage in time "breaks the relationship between cause and effect," the contamination of reality with dream produces a situation in which "the dreamer creates the world of which he himself is a part," and the work within the work confuses the levels of reality as well as the reader with the fictional character.[25]

Borges' own fiction not only includes numerous examples of these four devices; it leans heavily on them. Because the first procedure enumerated by Borges, the literary work within the literary work, is one that is employed to a great extent by the French practitioners of the nouveau roman (New Novel) as well as by Borges himself, a comparative study of the manner in which this device is handled would be revealing.

Reduced models of the work contained within itself, or "internal duplication," is sometimes referred to by modern French critics as mise en abyme. Originally referring to the emblem repeated in miniature within heraldic design, the term is also employed to describe a picture in which a figure holds a picture of itself in miniature which, in turn, holds a still smaller model of itself, theoretically ad infinitum. The term can also refer to the infinitely decreasing and more distant figures reflected in two facing mirrors. It has been used in one way or another for centuries; however, its purpose has varied considerably. The mise en abyme as a literary device was first described by André Gide, yet the device itself certainly is nothing new.[26] It has been used in one way or another for centuries; however, its purpose has varied considerably.

More anciently, the mise en abyme was employed as a device for reflecting the larger work in which it was contained or of allowing the characters belonging to the larger work to somehow understand their own actions and motives (e.g. Shakespeare's *Hamlet*: "The play's the thing wherein I'll catch the conscience of the king.") In other cases, e.g., Corneille's *L'illusion comique*, internal duplication has been used merely to create a surprise twist. In modern times, especially with reference to the French nouveau roman, the literary work within the literary work often serves the purpose of cutting the ties between the text and the external world, of having the text fold in on itself, so to speak. In this way, a work becomes an entirely self-sufficient world in itself. Bruce Morrissette comments:

> In its most recent stage in the novels and theoretical treatises of Jean Ricardou, the 'mise en abyme' does not seem to function either to reflect the work as though in a little mirror, or to give the fictional characters a means on their own level to watch themselves in operation, to judge themselves, to understand themselves...but rather to permit the text itself to attain new modalities, to distort the fictional space so that it folds in on itself, while severing all bonds between the novel and the everyday world. The novel thus becomes more self-sufficient...[27]

Jean Ricardou is, of course, a leading exponent and theorist of the French nouveau roman. His own comments on the role of internal duplication within the New Novel are revealing:

> I believe that most books of the New Novel contain, in one way or another, a mise en abyme, or

several, or even continual mises en abyme. This reduction, this image of the book within the book...has then, I believe...the peculiar function of emphasizing that the novel has no connection with anything other than itself. Instead of drawing attention to the everyday world in which we exist, it seems that there might be a sort of extremely concentrated will to draw attention toward the secret center of the book.[28]

The novels of Alain Robbe-Grillet contain abundant examples of internal duplication.[29] In *La Jalousie (Jealousy)*, 1957, both the novel-within-the-novel concerning European settlers in a tropical setting (the "African novel") and the picture calendar are firmly woven into the fabric of the novel. This "African novel" parallels the setting of *La Jalousie* itself, since it too deals with European planters in a tropical region. Beyond this fact, and more importantly, it is a topic of interest and conversation for A (the wife) and Franck, while it excludes the narrator-husband from conversation with them because he has not read it. Consequently, this novel-within-the-novel, while it may seem to reflect the larger work to some extent, this is not the reason it is included; the purpose of this mise en abyme is to serve as a direct trigger for many of the suspicions and fantasies of the narrator.

The very similarity of the situation in the mise en abyme to that in the larger novel is what provokes the husband-narrator, as he listens to snatches of conversation between his wife and Franck, into fantasizing about his wife's possible adultery with their neighbor. It is these fantasies which form a substantial part of the "action" of *La Jalousie*, so that the details from the "African novel" constitute an integral part of the structure of *La Jalousie* and act as a motivating force, as cause for at least part of the effect.

The same thing can be said about the illustration on the calendar; because it depicts a tropical port similar to the one to which the narrator's wife is taking a shopping trip with Franck, it sparks fantasies concerning them when the narrator-husband looks at it. These two examples of internal duplication in *La Jalousie*, then, are important to the world of this particular novel. It does, as Wheelock suggests, place the reader on the same level of reality as the characters in the novel. It is also a device through which the larger work refers to itself. One critic even sees the mysterious tune of the "second driver," a melody which wavers up and down and seems to stop in mid song only to start again, as a form of internal duplication in *La Jalousie*: "Let us say in passing that the analogy to music can become, as in Robbe-Grillet's *La Jalousie*, in which a native chant is described in terms that apply very obviously to the novel itself, an entirely conscious use of the 'mise en abyme'".[30]

An example of internal duplication in Borges, out of so many possibilities, is the story, "El milagro secreto" ("The Secret Miracle"), included in the collection *Ficciones*, in which there are three mises en abyme within those few pages. The very first sentence of the story refers to the dream of the protagonist, Jaromir Hladík, concerning a chess game:

> It was not being played by two individuals but by two illustrious families; the game had begun many centuries before; no one was capable of naming the forgotten prize, but it was rumored to be enormous and perhaps infinite; the pieces and the chessboard were in a secret tower; Jaromir (in the dream) was the firstborn son of one of the hostile families; the clocks were striking the hour for the undeferable move; the dreamer was running across the sands of a rainy desert and could not manage to remember the what the pieces or the laws of chess were. At this point, he awoke.

"The Secret Miracle," the story which contains the dream, concerns Jaromir Hladík, the Jewish Czech writer who is about to be executed by the Germans in World War II. Briefly stated, Hladík, awaiting execution, prays for God to grant him one year in which to complete his unfinished play *Los Enemigos* (*The Enemies*). This miracle is granted; when the command to fire is given the executioners, the physical world seems to come to a halt; a bee stands still in mid air, as though in a painting, a drop of rain that had fallen on Hladík's face stops rolling down his cheek to stay in place, the firing squad is frozen in place, the sergeant's mouth open... Hladík finally realizes that a year is going to pass in his mind during the brief interval between the command to fire and its execution. In this way, he is mentally able to finish the play.

The opening dream, which is covered in one short paragraph, contains many symbolic elements that could be analyzed, but suffice it to say that the dreamer's race against time for his move in the chess game is premonitory; it foreshadows Hladík's need to finish the play before the sands of time run out for him in life. The reference to the "forgotten prize" which is described as "enormous and perhaps infinite" could refer to Hladík's conviction that the plot of his play embodied "the chance to redeem (in a symbolic manner) what was fundamental in his life." This, certainly, is no mean prize. He tells God: "In order to conclude this play, which could justify my existence and justify You, I need one more year." The desert through which the dreamer runs is indicative of the sterility of his efforts thus far to complete the drama.

Borge's second device of fantastic literature, the "contamination" of reality with dream, should not be understood as being synonymous with the mere use of dreams in fiction. It specifically refers to an effect produced on the real world --whether the true real world or the "real" world lived in by fictional characters-- by the images of a dream. Coleridge's conjecture, dealt with in Borges' "La flor de Coleridge" ("Coleridge's Flower") on the results of a man's having dreamed he had been in Paradise and subsequent awakening with the flower presented to him in the dream still in his hand, is an example of what Borges was referring to. The first dream in "The Secret Miracle" does not alter reality in any concrete manner; it does not result in the "contamination of reality." But it certainly is a mise en abyme, an internal duplication of the larger work in which it is contained, and symbolically foreshadows that work.

Time is the subject matter of the chess dream as it is of the entire story.

The second mise en abyme in "The Secret Miracle" is Hladik's play, *Los Enemigos* (*The Enemies*), which is summarized by Borges in one paragraph. At the end of the summary we are informed that "The drama has not taken place; it is the circular delirium that is interminably lived and relived by Kubin" (p. 170). It is significant that the clock strikes seven as the sun sets and while a familiar Hungarian tune is heard during the first scene of the first act of the play, because these same elements are present during the last scene of the last act. This indicates that almost no time has passed from the beginning of the play to the end. Even though it would theoretically take two or three hours for *The Enemies* to be performed on a stage, the entire action is shown to take place in Kubin's fevered mind while the clock is striking seven.

Borges is demonstrating the contrast between the subjective time of the play's mad protagonist (corresponding to the time it would take to perform the play) and objective time: the brief moment during which his mind -- operating at high velocity-- conjures up those images.

The entire drama represents one brief moment of the protagonist's delirium: the moment during which the clock strikes seven and the Hungarian tune is heard. The play deals with time and is premonitory of the subjective year Hladík will live within the split second of objective time between the command to the firing squad and the execution of the command. This deformation of time, so frequent in Robbe-Grillet's novels and films and which has been termed "temps humain" ("human time")[31] by French critics, foreshadows the process which will permit Borges' fictional playwright to "live" one year during the lapse of a fraction of a second. His mind, like that of Kubin, the character in his play, operates at a pace will allow him to mentally accomplish what would normally require a year of his time.

This contrast between objective and subjective time, between clock time and personal time, is a phenomenon familiar to everyone. Thirty seconds under the dentist's drill is precisely 120 times shorter, in objective clock time, than an entire hour wining and dining in pleasant surroundings in the company of good friends. Yet those thirty seconds under the drill feel infinitely longer than that hour of pleasure, which slips by all too swiftly. Borges weaves the colorful, complex, multifaceted pattern of "The Secret Miracle" around this simple and familiar theme. He uncovers the magic of reality.

The third mise en abyme is, as was the first, a dream. The dream concerns Hladík's search for God in the Clementine Library and his final success. In the context of his prayer for another year of life, this would imply that his wish had been granted. This is confirmed when, in this magical dream, he is explicitly informed: "The time for your work has been granted." In the next sentence, the narrator states that Hladík remembered that the dreams of men belong to God, and that Maimonides wrote that the words of a dream are divine, when each word is separate and clear and are spoken by someone invisible. In addition to being merely premonitory then, this dream, this mise en abyme, serves, as Morrissette said with reference to the novels of Jean Ricardou, to cut the bonds between the work of fiction and prosaic reality, making the work more self-sufficient.

Or as Jean Ricardou said of the New Novel in general, it serves to draw our attention toward the "secret center" of the work. That secret center is, in "The Secret Miracle," the mystifying contrast between the two forms of time under which we all operate.

We have seen specific motives for internal duplication in Borges and in Robbe-Grillet. In both authors, the work of art within the work of art serves to foreshadow the events in the larger work, to provide a clue to the larger work's significance, or even to behave as a catalyst for the action in it. At the same time it insulates the work of fiction against the reality of the outside world and draws the reader into the special world, with its own self-sufficient laws, of the work of fiction. This technique is found throughout Robbe-Grillet's work. Referring specifically to *La maison de rendez-vous* (1965), in a statement which could apply equally well to most of Robbe-Grillet's work, Morrisette states:

> The nonrealism, or even the impossibility of the novel's content permits an emotionalized reading which is not, however, projected upon outside reality, fictional or otherwise. The criteria of the novel derive from this main principle; the work forms a functional universe in which time, space, causality, and all other coordinates obey internal rules entirely unrelated to classic plausibility ("Could this happen in real life?") (*Les romans...*, p. 241).

The critic describes a fictional world which not only refuses to imitate the real world but which flaunts its independence of the outside reality and which seeks to draw the reader into a unique and private universe. Robbe-Grillet himself has stated:

> In this new realism, it is no longer a question of verism at all. The little detail that "makes it [seem] real" no longer holds the novelist's attention, [either] in [contemplating] the spectacle of the world or in literature; what does strike him --and what is retained after quite a few of the avatars in which he writes-- from now on will be, on the contrary, the little detail that makes it [seem] false. (*Pour un nouveau roman*, 177-78).

The notion that the work of fiction owes no allegiance to facts or laws external to its own constitution is not something invented by the French New Novelists, of course.

This concept is basically that expressed as long ago as 1932 by Borges in his essay, "El arte narrativo y la magia" ("Narrative Art and Magic") The final paragraph encapsulates the essay:

> I'll attempt to sum up the above. I have distinguished between two causal processes: the natural one, which is the incessant result of uncontrollable and infinite operations; the magic one, in which the details, lucid and limited, prophecy. In the novel, I think the only possible honesty rests with the second [process]. Leave the first one for psychological simulation.[32]

Within the body of the essay, Borges explains that just one of the varieties of the genre of the novel, the time-consuming novel of character, "makes up or disposes of a concatenation of causes which supposedly do not differ from those of the real world." (*Discusión*, p. 88) He goes on to say however, that this procedure is not the usual one. Borges then states that this series of causes is not fitting for an action novel, for the short story or motion picture (which he characterizes as "the infinite spectacular novel that Hollywood composes"). These genres, he explains, are governed by magic, and magic, he tells us, is governed by sympathy, in that a link is established between entities which are distant from one another, the linkage being due to their having been close at one time ("contagious magic") or to their having an appearance that is similar in some way.

As examples of this second, "imitative," brand of magic, Borges speaks of the members of an Indian tribe who used to dance for days and nights on end wrapped in buffalo skins, with buffalo horns affixed to their heads, in order to assure the arrival of the buffalo herd. He also brings in the Australian aborigines who would cut their forearms, allowing them to bleed, so that the sky would "bleed" rain in imitation of their action (*Discusión*, pp. 88-89). Borges develops his discussion of magic by stating that this "dangerous harmony," this "frenzied and precise causality" operates in the novel too. He explains that although the fear that some dreadful act may be brought into being merely by mentioning its name is inoperative in the real world of modern Western civilization, this is not the case in a novel. Every single episode, in a carefully constructed plot, produces reverberations. (Ibid. 89-90).

While he does not specifically apply this reasoning to internal duplication, there is no reason to believe that he would exclude it. In this light, the mise en abyme would not only place the reader on the same level of reality with the fictional characters, thereby effectively plunging the reader into the self-contained fictional world of a particular piece, but in addition can serve as a magical cause for other events within this fictional world.

Certainly, this is what occurs in Robbe-Grillet's *La Jalousie* as well as in his novels in general; this is what takes place in Borges' "El milagro secreto." Just as the buffalo dance brings the buffalo, as the bleeding "causes" the rain, the juxtaposition of objective and subjective time that is present in *Los Enemigos,* the play within the story "El milagro secreto," sympathetically "causes" the identical juxtaposition in the larger work. The delirious imaginings of the protagonist of *Los Enemigos* "cause" the author of this play, who is also the protagonist of "El Milagro Secreto," to imagine deliriously that he is living an extra year in a fraction of a second. Or is it the other way around? Does the type of mind that is subject to delirium write a play like *Los Enemigos*? But this would not be magic; it would correspond to situations in the real world and, as Borges has said, would be best left for "psychological simulation." Returning to magic, then, the "African novel" and the calendar in Robbe-Grillet's *La Jalousie* are the causes, in part, of the fantasies in the protagonist's mind.

It is clear that the internal duplication practiced by French New Novelists had been effectively employed earlier by Jorge Luis Borges. It is equally clear that the reasons for employing this device, according to theoretical treatises by

French novelists and critics, and interviews with them -- reasons having to do with making the work of art independent of the outside world and with bringing the reader into the closed world of the work of fiction-- have been operating in the works of Borges for a very long time.

Furthermore, it appears that another motive for utilizing the mise en abyme is present in Borges as well as in the French New Novel; that of producing magic. Yet magic, as described by the Argentinean writer Borges, is really what the French New Novelists are talking about when they speak of a "functional universe in which time, space, causality, and all other coordinates obey internal rules entirely unrelated to classic plausibility." The literature of this type, found in Borges and in Robbe-Grillet, is a form of magic realism.

WORKS CONSULTED

Borges, Jorge Luis. *Discusión*. Buenos Aires: Emecé, 1964.
_____. *Ficciones*. Buenos Aires: Emecé, 1956.
Morrissette, bruce. "Un Héritage d'André Gide: La Duplication intérieur, "*Comparative Literature Studies*, vol. 7, no. 2 (June 1971), 125-42.
_____. *The Novels of Robbe-Grillet*, translated from the French, revised, updated, and expanded, with a Foreword by Roland Barthes. Ithaca and London: Cornell University Press, 1975.
_____. *Les Romans de Robbe-Grillet*, Préface de Roland Barthes, nouvelle édition augmentée. Paris: Les éditions de Minuit, 1963.
Passos, Carlos Alberto. Synopsis of Borges' lecture of September 2, 1949. In newspaper *El País*. Montevideo, Uruguay, September 3, 1949.
Robbe-Grillet, Alain. *La Jalousie* 1957.
_____. *La Maison de rendez-vous* 1965.
_____. *Pour un nouveau roman*. Paris: Les Editions de Minuit, 1963.
Rodríguez Monegal, Emir. "Jorge Luis Borges y la literatura fantástica," *Número*, vol.1, no.5 (November-December 1949), 448-455.

CHAPTER 4

BORGES AND THE FRENCH "NEW NOVEL":

THE UNMEDIATED EXPERIENCE

Jorge Luis Borges is blind while Alain Robbe-Grillet is visually oriented. Borges produces highly compressed poetry, short fiction, literary criticism and philosophical essays, whereas Robbe-Grillet is an exponent of the nouveau roman (the so-called French "new novel") and of the ciné-roman ("movie novel"). Yet in spite of the apparent gulf between the anglophile Argentine and the Frenchman there exists an appreciable although camouflaged common ground. The more obvious points of contact between the two authors are the highly labyrinthine aspects of their art, the allusions to or reworkings of mythological themes, and the preoccupation with and manipulation of time and space. There are, however, less immediately obvious similarities. It is on these more covert --and therefore more intriguing-- affinities that this essay will concentrate.

"El milagro secreto" ("The Secret Miracle") of Borges is narrated in the third person and ostensibly belongs to the genre of the fantastic tale. The protagonist, Jaromir Hladík, is a Czech-Jewish writer about to be executed by the invading Germans during World War II. The story is metaphysical in that God allows Hladík to live for one year in the interval between the moment in which the command to fire is given the firing squad and that in which the soldiers actually carry out the command. (The entire physical universe comes to a halt for one year while Hladík's mind continues to function, allowing him to finish his play.)[33] Hladík had asked God for the extra year in which to complete his drama, *Los enemigos* (*The Enemies*), judging that its completion alone would justify his existence and therefore justify his Creator.

It is this play-within-the-story, *The Enemies*, summed

up by Borges in one single paragraph, which provides a striking parallel to Robbe-Grillet's novel *La Jalousie* (*Jealousy*), despite the fact that the novel is written in a most unorthodox and experimental style. The reader only gradually comes to realize that it is being narrated in the first person, since the first person singular pronoun "I" is never employed, nor does the narrator ever refer to himself.

Until the reader becomes acclimated to the style, the narrative does not seem to follow a straight line in time or space. One finally becomes aware that *La Jalousie* is an attempt at reproducing that which the invisible narrator sees, hears, and imagines. The reader, in seeing and hearing exactly what the husband-narrator sees and hears, even when these perceptions are distorted through jealousy to the point of exaggeration and pure fantasy, becomes the husband-narrator.

In order to investigate the similarities between Robbe-Grillet's *La Jalousie* and Hladík's *The Enemies*, the briefly-summarized play within Borges' "The Secret Miracle," we need to examine the concise review of the play provided by Borges:

This drama observed the unities of time, place and action; it took place in Hradcany, in Baron von Roemerstadt's library, on one of the last afternoons of the nineteenth century. In the first scene of the first act, a stranger is visiting Roemerstadt. (A clock strikes seven, a setting sun's intensity inflames the window panes, a passionate and familiar Hungarian melody is carried on the air.) Other visitors follow this one; Roemerstadt does not know the people who importune him, but he has the uncomfortable feeling of having seen them before, perhaps in a dream. They all flatter him to the utmost, but it is noticeable --at first to the audience, later to the Baron himself-- that they secretly are enemies, conspiring to ruin him. Roemerstadt manages to fend off or frustrate their complex intrigues; in the dialogue, mention is made of his fiancée, Julia von Weidenau, and of one Jaroslav Kubin, who at one time had importuned her with declarations of love. This Kubin has now gone mad and believes he is Roemerstadt... The dangers become more threatening; Roemerstadt, at the end of the second act, finds it necessary to kill one of the conspirators. The third and final act begins. The incongruities gradually increase: actors who seemed to have been already eliminated from the plot return; the man slain by Roemerstadt returns for one instant. Someone points out the fact that it has not grown dark: the clock strikes seven, the western sun reflects upon the tall window panes, a passionate Hungarian melody is carried on the air. The first speaker appears and repeats the words he pronounced in the first scene of the first act. Roemerstadt speaks to him without the least surprise; the spectator realizes that Roemerstadt is the wretched Jaroslav Kubin. The drama has not taken place: it is the circular delirium which Kubin unendingly lives and relives. (*Ficciones*, 162-63). [34]

One might conceive of "The Secret Miracle" as the fictionalization of a metaphysical problem in the form of a short story, while considering *La Jalousie* an artificially and artistically-induced emotion in the form of a novel. These are two very different entities, yet we can discover striking similarities between the two works.

The last phrase of Borges' synopsis of the play, "it is the circular delirium which Kubin unendingly lives and relives," taken with no change whatever save that of substituting the person of the husband-narrator of *La Jalousie* for Kubin, would apply equally well to a summary of Robbe-Grillet's novel. In fact, Bruce Morrissette's reference to the constitution of this novel is similar to this last phrase of Borges' concerning "The Enemies" even with regard to his choice of language. Morrisette writes, "La composition de *La Jalousie* est donc commandée par la vision d'un homme, d'un jaloux qui progresse dans le temps, c'est-a-dire vit les épisode, mais aussi les réexamine, les compare, les interroge et surtout les modifie, les change au gré de son imagination" ("The composition of *Jealousy*, then, is dominated by the vision of one man, a jealous man who progresses through time, that is to say lives the episodes, but also re-examines them, compares them, questions them and above all modifies them, changes them in accordance with his imagination"). (Morrisette, 114).

Kubin's living and reliving is equivalent to the living and re-examining, questioning and modifying the episodes referred to by Morrisette. An objection could be raised at this point: the narrator of *La Jalousie* is said to live the episodes literally before modifying them in his imagination, while it seems that the living and reliving mentioned by Borges is merely a figure of speech for pure imagining, since it is a "delirium" that he lives, and since Borges tells us explicitly that the drama "has not taken place." It might appear that the entire play reviewed by Borges represents nothing more than a figment of a jealous imagination, whereas the events in *La Jalousie* represent a combination: actual events occurring in linear, objective time plus the imaginary or distortedly-perceived events taking place entirely in the imagination.

However, the statement indicating the drama did not take place could be applied equally as well to Robbe-Grillet's novel, either as a whole or considering only certain episodes (the imagined adultery and the accident scene, which almost certainly take place only in the mind of the narrator). Conversely, Borges' statement with regard to the play must not be taken at face value, since in order for Kubin to "live and relive" his delirium, he must first exist (fictionally, of course, as does the husband-narrator of *La Jalousie*) and have known Julia von Weidenau as well as the Baron in order to have fantasies concerning them. In addition, Kubin perforce had to know of their engagement and have been in love with her himself in order to have had a motive for being insanely jealous. The problem, then, is only apparent and is based on Borges' inaccuracy as a reviewer in stating that the drama did not take place. Even if nothing else were actually perceived by Kubin, at least Baron Roemerstadt and Julia Weidenau were.

One might protest that even though the basic idea underpinning the plots of both Hladík's play, *The Enemies*, and Robbe-Grillet's novel, *La Jalousie* (if a plot is conceded to the latter) is practically identical, the more important aspect to be examined is the techniques of expressing this basic theme, that it is the structure of *La Jalousie* which is the most significant factor to consider.

It is indeed the structure of *La Jalousie* which provides its uniqueness and its power to place the reader directly within the husband-narrator, seeing with the narrator's eyes, hearing with the narrator's ears, interpreting the impressions received with the narrator's mind, this disturbed mind which forces the narrator (and, therefore, the reader) to distort the obsessively repeated memory images and to fantasize.

This technique of Robbe-Grillet, repeatedly flooding the reader's mind with the perceptions and the interpretations of the narrator as directly received, produces in the reader the emotion of jealousy. Since the reader never sees the narrator, but sees with the narrator's eyes as though the reader were inside the narrator's body looking out, the reader becomes the narrator. The words on the printed page are not felt to be pronounced by a third person or even by a first person, in the usual sense of the term. As h/she progresses, the reader begins to feel that these words are not pronounced at all, but that they combine to form experiences that the reader directly undergoes.

La Jalousie confuses the reader at first because of the seeming chaos of time and place, the sudden shifts of scene, scenes which are repeated with slight, almost imperceptible changes initially, increasing as the novel progresses. This confusion comes about as a result of the reader's lack of acclimatization to Robbe-Grillet's technique. The reader is accustomed to the traditional framework of the novel: a linear sequence of events starting at X and ending at Y.

Furthermore, the reader depends upon a narrator, whether third person or first or even second, who informs the reader explicitly that a particular set of words is pronounced while others are merely thought, and that certain scenes are viewed as they take place while others are remembered or imagined. When the reader ceases to resist and allows him/herself to receive the impressions bombarding him/her, at that point the reader magically becomes the narrator.

We, the reader-as-narrator or reader-as-protagonist (as opposed to the traditional reader-as-listener) peer through the blinds (the jalousie) and see the motionless workmen in the fields in daylight, then abruptly find ourselves observing "our" wife (whose name is given only as the initial A) with the neighbor (Franck) at table in the evening, then see A and Franck in the hotel, and finally, after several pages, once more see through the blinds the motionless workmen in the fields in daylight. It is at this point that we realize that we are standing at the window watching the laborers, but that our mind's eye repeatedly shifts to scenes remembered or imagined.

The repetitions of events as well as shifts of scene are no more than displacements of the mind which wavers in its concentration on scenes remembered from the past and imagined scenes projected into the future (dinner, the hotel) to attention to that which is presently before the eyes (the laborers). The workmen seem not to have moved or scarcely to have done so because the time expended in remembering and imagining is not objective time, but subjective time. For this reason, after "seeing" a remembered or imagined episode which might seem to cover hours or days, only a fraction of a second might have elapsed when the mind again begins to interpret the data actually before the eyes.

In assigning the proper importance to structure in *La Jalousie*, the temptation is to dismiss out of hand any comparison between "The Enemies" and *La Jalousie*. *La Jalousie* is a novel while *The Enemies* is a play. The author of the novel is Alain Robbe-Grillet, but the author of *The Enemies* is not Borges; he is Jaromir Hladík, the Czech playwright invented by Borges as the protagonist of the short story "The Secret Miracle."

The main problem concerning any comparison of structure or technique with respect to Hladík's play and

Robbe-Grillet's novel lies in there being no copy of the play available to us. Consequently we cannot directly experience the play as we can the novel. We have only Borges' cursory summary of the play with which to work.

If Robbe-Grillet's manuscript of *La Jalousie* had disappeared before publication but after the manuscript had been read by Bruce Morrissette, and the only information accessible to us concerning *La Jalousie* were a plot summary of it presented in a linear manner by Morrissette --only his plot summary, not his explication and analysis-- then we would have a fitting basis for comparison of the two works, still bearing in mind that Borges' summary of *The Enemies* is brief to the utmost, while Morrissette's plot summary of *La Jalousie* is highly detailed (116-22).[35]

The only other method of creating a solid foundation for a comparison of structure and technique in general concerning *The Enemies* and *La Jalousie* would be to discover the "lost" manuscript of Hladík's play. This is impossible. Nevertheless, even in the fleeting outline of this theatrical piece provided by Borges there are allusions to and even descriptions of its structure and techniques.

As readers of "The Secret Miracle" we know that when the last scene of the last act of *The Enemies* has concluded, the audience of this play realizes that the drama it has witnessed on stage is merely the "circular delirium" repeatedly and infinitely experienced in the mind of the obsessively jealous protagonist. We, the readers of "The Secret Miracle," know this because Borges has expressly informed us of this fact. Yet beyond this bare statement of fact, Borges has also briefly mentioned the techniques employed by Hladík to ensure that the hypothetical audience, which would have to depend on what it sees and hears on the stage, is made unequivocally aware of this.

Borges tells us that the series of events in the play gradually take on an ever increasing air of unreality. At first, the sense of unreality is slight, though definite, e.g. Roemerstadt is not acquainted with his visitors, but uncomfortably experiences a sort of déja vu upon being confronted by them

(p. 163). In the conversation, it is mentioned that Kubin has lost his mind and believes himself to be Roemerstadt. The oneiric quality of Roemerstadt's visitors, along with the discomfort they produce, the allusion to madness and confusion of identity, all lead to a delirious quality which would surely produce uneasiness among the audience. The identical delirious quality and uneasiness are conveyed to the reader of *La Jalousie* by means of the sudden shifts of scene, as well as by the repetition of certain episodes, especially when particular details suffer mutation or distortion each time the scene is repeated.

Borges tells us that the dangers become more threatening. He delves into no details about these dangers, but we must assume that the audience would witness the events to which Borges alludes. In so doing, the spectators would become subject to an increasing malaise. The menacing occurrences, which the audience would not yet realize are imaginary, serve the same purpose as the steadily mounting details of "evidence" of imagined adultery perceived by the reader-narrator of *La Jalousie*. Roemerstadt, we are told, finds it necessary to kill a conspirator. When we see, in *La Jalousie*, A and Franck in the burning truck, the narrator "sees" this scene in his imagination because he wants to; it is a wish-fulfillment daydream. He too finds it necessary to kill conspirators; he does so in his imagination, but so does Roemerstadt, or rather Kubin, as we finally learn, in *The Enemies*.

In the last act of *The Enemies* the incongruities gradually increase. This is exactly what occurs toward the climax of *La Jalousie*, and in both cases is the result of an ever increasing mental disturbance. More specifically, the spectators of the play witness the return of actors who had seemed to have been dropped from the action of the play, including the man murdered by Roemerstadt. The first speaker appears and repeats the words he articulated in the first act of the first scene. This process is strikingly analogous to that of the seemingly incoherent repetition of scenes and conversations in *La Jalousie*. What is more, it signifies, as in the novel, that the repetition is actually an obsessive review of events in the mind of the protagonist. This fact is confirmed when the audience of *The Enemies* notices that Roemerstadt speaks to the murdered man with no trace of astonishment. No astonishment is produced in the mind of the narrator of *La Jalousie* either, just as there would be no surprise in anyone's mind when mentally reviewing past incidents, since one is aware that these "repetitions" are not present in objective time or in the physical world at the moment of remembering.

The jealous husband of *La Jalousie* continues to return to the perception of the field hands after experiencing intervening memories or fantasies of his wife and Franck. This process is analogous to the procedure in *The Enemies* in which the sight of the setting sun and the sound of the Hungarian tune and the appearance of the first actor who speaks his first words occur both at the beginning and once more at the conclusion of the play. In neither work is it a question of actual repetition.

In *La Jalousie* the intermittent view of the workmen is an anchor to the present which allows the reader to become aware that the surrounding scenes are being remembered or imagined while the narrator is actually observing the laborers at present. In *The Enemies* the series of repetitions at the end of Hladík's drama make patent to the spectators that no objective time has transpired from the beginning of the tragedy through to the final curtain; the intervening scenes take place in Roemerstadt-Kubin's mind, partially through reverie and partially through fantasy. In both the novel and the play, then, there is a circular and unending series of delirious fantasy interrupted by a spasmodic return to observation of the present.

Morrisette has said of Robbe-Grillet's novels in general that their goal is "non d'analyser, mais de créer la psychologie, et de l'imposer au lecteur par une écriture objective" ("not to analyze, but to create the psychology, and to impose it on the reader through objective writing") (p. 114). This is certainly true with respect to the achievement of *La*

Jalousie in which the reader is bombarded with the actual sensations undergone by the protagonist with no explanatory interference from any source, be it first person or third, omniscient or limited narrator. The sensations are experienced directly and we, as readers, have to sort them out and interpret them for ourselves just as we do in our personal non-reading lives.

The brief synopsis of Hladík's drama that Borges provides indicates than any audience present at that theatrical performance would be just as directly subject to the experiences undergone by the protagonist as is the reader of *La Jalousie*. Perhaps the audience would be even more directly affected because of the visual element and the immediacy of a stage presentation as opposed to reading the printed words in the pages of a novel.

The similarity between the novel and the play would have been even greater, of course, if the protagonist of Hladík's play did not appear on stage, but therein lies the difference between a performed play and a novel. Still, it is questionable as to whether we really see the protagonist, Kubin, since we really see Roemerstadt, which is the way the deluded Kubin sees himself. Be that as it may, Morrisette's assertion regarding the process of creating, rather than analyzing, the workings of a particular mental process, and then imposing that process on the reader is equally true of Hladík's play (changing "reader" to "audience") as it is to Robbe-Grillet's novel. Morrisette's statement referring specifically to *La Jalousie*, indicating that its object is to "créer objectivement... le 'contenu mental' d'un narrateur jaloux" ("create objectively... the 'mental contents' of a jealous narrator") (p. 114) would be equally applicable to *The Enemies* as well.

Even the detail of the use of the sun's position in *The Enemies* as a reference point is strikingly analogous to the constant use of the sun's position in *La Jalousie* for precisely the same purpose. In Hladík's play, however, the setting sun as well as the clock which strikes seven serves as a liaison between the play and the short story in which it is contained, "The Secret Miracle." In addition, the sun and the clock in the play serve as symbols. They fulfill both the linking and the symbolic function in that they represent the short time left to Hladík to finish the play in which these symbols appear (his sun is metaphorically setting).

As symbols these phenomena would be allowed no point of contact with *La Jalousie*. Robbe-Grillet has frequently repudiated the use of symbolism.[36] Nevertheless, he has agreed that objects may function as supports or props for emotions, which is another way of saying they can act as what has been termed "objective correlatives," and therefore are able to bear some psychic charge, as does the centipede in *La Jalousie*.[37]

In *The Enemies* the setting sun, the clock and the Hungarian melody might well, for all we know, be developed in the play in such a manner as to be objective correlatives or "supports," which would place them in the same category as the centipede and other objects employed for the identical supporting purpose by Robbe-Grillet. It is also curious to note the way in which the Hungarian melody of *The Enemies* resembles, in its mysterious function, the unusual tune sung by the native "second driver" in *La Jalousie*.[38]

It is significant that it is *The Enemies*, the play within the Borgesian short story, "The Secret Miracle," rather than the short story itself, that we have compared with Robbe-Grillet's novel *La Jalousie*. The work of art within the work of art, internal duplication, is a persistent and well developed device in the production of both Borges and Robbe-Grillet.

In *La Jalousie* both the novel concerning European settlers in tropical Africa and the calendar bearing the picture of the port are firmly woven into the fabric of the novel. The "roman africain" ("African novel"), because of the parallels it presents to the milieu of *La Jalousie*, the novel in which it is contained, and because it provides a topic of interest and discussion for A and Franck to the exclusion of the narrator-husband, who has not read it, directly foments many of the suspicions and fantasies of the narrator.

The picture on the calendar excites fantasies as well,

since it depicts the port in which Franck and A are (were, will be) visiting together. Details heard in the conversations about the African novel become incorporated into the fantasies of the narrator concerning his wife and Franck. The employment of the story-within-the-story in *La Jalousie* is far from gratuitous; it constitutes an integral part of the structure of the novel and serves as a motivating force.

Borges may have forgotten, during his interview with Richard Burgin, his original motives for including that synopsis of the play *The Enemies* in "The Secret Miracle." [39] He might even have been consciously unaware of them. Just as likely he was speaking tongue in cheek; this playfulness would not be out of character for Borges. In any event, whether Borges' motives were conscious or unconscious, it is clear that *The Enemies* foreshadows the main event of "The Secret Miracle," the short story in which it appears.

While neither motivational nor an integral element of the plot, as is the African novel with relation to *La Jalousie*, *The Enemies* is not gratuitous either. It is premonitory of the fate of Hladík, its author. As such, it provides a richer, more esthetic whole for "The Secret Miracle." *The Enemies* depicts events occurring during the three acts which would necessitate two or three hours for the play to be performed in a theater. This block of time represents the subjective time of the insanely jealous Kubin; the events only seem to him to take this long. When we find that the play represents a "circular delirium" imagined by the madman, and that the entire event occurs while the sun is in the act of setting, the clock is striking seven, and a Hungarian melody is being played, we realize that in objective time only a fraction of a second passes between the beginning of the delirium and its end.

This deliberate juxtaposition of objective and subjective time —clock time and human time-- parallels and foreshadows the process which will allow Hladík to "live" one full year (in his mind) in the brief moment between the time in which the firing squad is ordered to fire and the instant in which the command is carried out.

Jaromir Hladík's play, so parsimoniously touched on by Borges, not only treats the identical theme upon which is based Robbe-Grillet's novel *La Jalousie*, but also employs the same techniques. Whereas the short stories of Jorge Luis Borges avoid creating emotion in the reader (see Chapter 1), Jaromir Hladík (Borges' creation) and Robbe-Grillet, on the stage and on the printed page respectively, oblige the spectator/reader to undergo directly the visual and mental experiences of the protagonist until the same emotion is produced in the former as that obtaining in the latter. In both cases the spectator/reader is situated within the protagonist and, for the duration of the artistic experience, becomes him. In the play as well as in the novel, the constant repetition and shuffling of scenes result in the artistic recreation of a constantly repeated circular delirium.

One disparity in this comparison, a trifling one, is that we are comparing the actual novel written by Alain Robbe-Grillet, who exists in the real world, with a mere synopsis of a play written by Jaromir Hladík who lives only in the fictional world of Jorge Luis Borges.

WORKS CONSULTED

Bersani, Leo. "Toward an Esthetic of Disappearance? Narrative Murder," in *Balzac to Beckett: Center and Circumference in French Fiction*. New York: Oxford University Press, 1970.

Borges, Jorge Luis. *Ficciones*. (Third printing, 1961). Buenos Aires: Emecé, 1956.

Burgin, Richard. *Conversations With Jorge Luis Borges*. New York: Holt, Rinehart & Winston, 1969.

Morrissette, Bruce. *Les Romans de Robbe-Grillet*. Préface de Roland Barthes. Paris: Editions de Minuit, 1963.

Robbe-Grillet, Alain. *Les Gommes*. Paris: Editions de Minuit, 1953.

_____. *La Jalousie*. Paris: Editions de Minuit, 1957.

CHAPTER 5

BORGES AND THE FRENCH "NEW NOVEL":

THE READER AS ACCOMPLICE

An inept detective wanders through the streets of a labyrinthine city in an attempt to find a killer. After a great deal of lucubration, after much investigation, the detective himself falls into a trap and is victimized. This plot summary would apply equally well (equally superficially) to "La muerte y la brújula" ("Death and the Compass") (1942), the story by Argentine writer Jorge Luis Borges and to *Les Gommes* (*The Erasers*) (1953), the novel by the practitioner of the French nouveau roman ("New Novel") Alain Robbe-Grillet.

In the story by Borges the city takes on the appearance of a spider web in the center of which Lonrot, the detective, perishes at the hands of the gunman Red Scharlach. In Robbe-Grillet's novel the investigator, Wallas, loses himself in the confusion of the canal-crossed circular city until he himself becomes the killer he is seeking.

(Garinati, a professional killer, fires at Dupont at seven-thirty in the evening. Dupont is not killed although Garinati is not aware of this. Dupont is hidden by his friends. The police believe that Dupont is dead although they cannot find the body. Dupont returns to his house the following night, looking for important papers. The detective arrives at Dupont's home some minutes later. Upon seeing Dupont he believes he has trapped the killer. Dupont thinks the detective is the murderer returning to finish the job. Dupont raises his gun and is killed by the detective exactly twenty-four hours after the supposed murder.)

Less superficially, the fact that the bullet is delayed by an entire day in taking the life of the victim links *The Erasers* to a different Borges story, "El milagro secreto"

("The Secret Miracle") (1943). In this story Jaromir Hladík, the Czech-Jewish writer, is granted one year by God between the moment in which the German sergeant gives the firing squad the order to shoot and the moment in which the command is executed. During this time, "el universo físico se detuvo" ("the physical universe stopped").

Hladík had prayed for that year's interval in order to complete his unfinished play, *Los enemigos* (*The Enemies*), The narrator explains the miracle: "God was working a secret miracle for him [Hladík]: the German bullet would kill him, at the correct time, but in his mind a year would elapse between the order and the execution of the order" (*Ficciones*, 166). Of course, this can be conceptualized as the acceleration of the playwright's mental processes which enables him to accomplish, in the fraction of a second that exists between the order to fire and its execution, what ordinarily would necessitate a whole year.

However one interprets the miracle, a brief plot summary of "The Secret Miracle" would be almost identical with the synopsis actually provided for *The Erasers* by Robbe-Grillet himself in the prière d'insérer: "Car le livre est justement le récit des vingt-quatre heures qui s'écoulent entre ce coup de pistolet et cette mort, le temps que la balle a mis pour parcourir trois ou quatre metres --vingt-quatre heures 'en trop'" ("For the book is no more nor less than the story of twenty-four hours `extra'"). With no change save that of converting the twenty-four hours into one year, this statement would apply equally well (and just as superficially) to "The Secret Miracle."

These "twenty-four hours 'extra' (or 'too many')" are dramatically reinforced in *The Erasers* by the detective's watch stopping at the exact moment Garinati fires at Dupont (7:50 P.M.) to start again only after the victim is actually killed twenty-four hours later by the detective. It is difficult to overlook the framing function of this detail as analogous to the clock's striking seven in Hladík's play *The Enemies* at the beginning and then again at the end of the drama, to demonstrate that the entire event portrayed in the play represents a brief moment in clock time during which the deranged protagonist imagines the action.

Stepping back from the specific similarities of Robbe-Grillet's *The Erasers*, Borges' "The Secret Miracle," and the play contained within it, *The Enemies*, it is apparent that the fiction of both authors share several characteristics in general terms: labyrinths and labyrinthine situations; the manipulation of time; police narratives; internal duplication or mise en abyme (the work-of-art within the work-of-art); allusions to or reworkings of myths (Robbe-Grillet's *The Erasers*, for example, is a sort of reworking of the Oedipus myth while Borges' "La muerte y la brújula" ["Death and the Compass"] has many points of contact with the myth of the Minotaur).

In addition, a technique which is an integral part of Robbe-Grillet's novelistic and cinematographic production --the repetition of scenes-- is not found in Borges' stories, although the process is described by Borges in his brief résumé of the play (*The Enemies*) within the story "The Secret Miracle."

All these characteristics are manifestations of one single idea. In his essay, "El arte narrativo y la magia" ("Narrative Art and Magic"), Borges affirms that the "secret subject matter" of Edgar Allen Poe's *Narrative of A. Gordon Pym* (1838), is the fear and vilification of the color white. The novel concerns some fictional tribes living in the Antarctic regions, among limitless whiteness, and who have suffered the depredations of white men and the terrors of white storms (snow storms). White is, Borges tells us, anathema for those tribes; he confesses the same is true for the reader as well by the end of the last chapter.

The book has two subjects, he writes; one, concerning a seafaring adventure, which is immediate, and another, "infalible, sigiloso y creciente" ("infallible, secret, and growing"), which is only brought to light at the end. Referring to the secrecy of the theme, Borges says: "Nombrar un objeto, dicen que dijo Mallarmé, es suprimir las tres cuartas partes del goce del poema, que reside en la felicidad de ir adivinando: el sueño es sugerirlo" (*Discusión*, 86). ("To name an object, they say that Mallarmé said, is to suppress three quarters of the enjoyment of the poem, which resides in the joy of solving a riddle; the dream is to suggest it"). At least as long ago as 1932, then, Borges was aware of the reader's pleasure in not having everything explicitly set before him/her, in being allowed to use his or her powers of deduction.

The singular appeal of the detective narrative lies in the fact that it permits the reader to participate in the solution of the mystery. As a result, the reader becomes an active participant who very often reaches his or her own conclusions even before the detective does. This fact adds another dimension to the enjoyment of literature: pride in accomplishment. Placing the detective stories and novels of these two authors to one side, this pride in accomplishment on the part of the reader is applicable to a large sector of the work of Borges and Robbe-Grillet. After all, labyrinths require reader participation and afford the same sense of elation at finding Ariadne's thread that solving a crime does. The repetition of scenes forms a maze in time rather than in space; the viewers of a Robbe-Grillet film (e.g. *Last Year in Marienbad*) participate, as they attempt to extract a linear plot from this temporal labyrinth (as do the readers of his novels) to the same extent as the hypothetical audience of Hladík's play.

Allusions to myths or their re-elaboration also require detective work; the reader is obliged to discover, to h/her great satisfaction, that a myth is involved, and then must determine precisely which myth it is. Even the mise en abyme or internal duplication may behave as a "clue" which the reader can first recognize as such and then utilize as a key for understanding the entire work in which it is contained (e. g. *The Enemies*, we are informed, is merely a circular delirium; the drama has not taken place. This forms a nexus with the story "The Secret Miracle" in which it is contained in that it foreshadows the miracle which takes place entirely within Hladík's imagination.)

The common denominator of all these facets of both writers' works --and this is significant-- the common denominator is the challenge hurled at the reader to take part in the creative process. Borges' interest in the concept of the reader as writer can be traced at least as far back as 1932 when, in the essay "Las versiones homéricas" ("Translations of Homer"), he speaks of the difficulty of translating a text written in an ancient language. In discussing the differing translations of Homer, along with their advantages and disadvantages, Borges suggests that the difference depends on the manner in which the translators read Homer. He will express this idea more directly in his "Nota sobre (hacia) Bernard Shaw" ("Note on (toward) Bernard Shaw") (1951): "Una literatura difiere de la otra, ulterior o anterior, menos por el texto que por la manera de ser leída..." ("One literature differs from another which is earlier or later, less because of the text than because of the way it is read...") (*Otras inquisiciones*, 202).

This concept takes on additional ramifications in the story "Pierre Menard, autor del Quijote" ("Pierre Menard, Author of Don Quixote") (1939). In this piece of fiction, a twentieth-century Frenchman manages to write several selections from *Don Quixote* using the identical words that had been used in Cervantes' text. The narrator declares that Cervantes' text and that of Menard are "verbalmente idénticos, pero el segundo es casi infinitamente más rico" ("verbally identical, but that the second is almost infinitely richer"). He adds: "Menard (acaso sin quererlo) ha enriquecido mediante una técnica nueva, el arte detenido y rudimentario de la lectura: la técnica del anacronismo deliberado y de las atribuciones erróneas" ("Menard [perhaps accidentally] has enriched, by means of a new technique, the slow and rudimentary art of reading: the technique of the deliberate anachronism and of erroneous attributions") (*Ficciones*, 56).

Although this is said ironically and with reference to the eccentric labors of Pierre Menard, it contains a germ of truth: the modern reader who reads the *Quixote* is not reading the same book that was read by a person of the seventeenth century. Each person brings to the text his or her peculiar mentality and experience. The same can be said, up to a point, of two neighbors who read the same novel.

In this context it is interesting to note that in his essay, "La supersticiosa ética del lector" ("The Superstitious Ethics of the Reader") (1930), Borges declares, "there are no more readers, in the ingenuous sense of the word, left: everyone is a potential critic" (*Discusión*, 47). Written two years previous to "Las versiones homéricas," it already suggests that the reader as mere reader, that is, as passive recipient of the writer's ideas, is foreign to Borges' thoughts.

Borges elaborates on this theme in the story (or series of fictitious book reviews) entitled "Examen de la obra de Herbert Quain" ("Examination of the Work of Herbert Quain"), dating from 1911. The fictitious Quain states, "No hay europeo...que no sea un escritor, en potencia o en acto." ("There is no European... who is not a writer, potentially or actually.") The narrator goes on to explain:

> Afirmaba también que de las diversas felicidades que puede ministrar la literatura, la más alta era la invención. Ya que no todos son capaces de esa felicidad, muchos habrán de contentarse con simulacros. Para esos "imperfectos escritores", cuyo nombre es legión, Quain redactó los ocho relatos del libro *Statements*. Cada uno de ellos prefigura o promete un buen argumento, voluntariamente frustrado por el autor. Alguno --no el mejor-- insinúa dos argumentos. El lector, distraído por la vanidad, cree haberlos inventado (*Ficciones*. p. 83).

> He also affirmed that of the different kinds of happiness literature can provide, the highest was invention. Since not everyone is capable of that happiness, many will have to content themselves with pretense. For those "imperfect writers" whose name is legion, Quain wrote the eight stories of the book

Statements. Each one of them foreshadows or promises a good plot, purposely thwarted by the author. One of them --not the best-- insinuates two plots. The reader, distracted by vanity, believes he has invented them.

April March, the novel by Quain described by Borges' narrator, has a certain similarity to several works by Robbe-Grillet, e.g. the novels *La Jalousie* (1957), *Dans le Labyrinthe* (1959), *La Maison de rendez-vous* (1965), *Projets pour une révolution a New York* (1970), and the film-novels *L'Anée dernière a Marienbad* (1961), and *Glissements progressifs du plaisir* (1974). The similarity is in the technique of presenting scenes that take place (possibly take place) before several other scenes shown previously and which contradict other scenes. In Robbe-Grillet's works as well as in Quain's *April March*, these scenes represent episodes which are merely possible and which compete with other, equally possible episodes. The narrator of "Examen de la obra de Herbert Quain" states that "Nadie, al juzgar esa novela, se niega a descubrir que es un juego; es licito recordar que el autor no la consideró nunca otra cosa" (*Ficciones*, 79). ("No one, upon judging this novel, refuses to discover that it is a game; it should be remembered that the author never considered it anything else.") It is a game, one in which the reader is allowed to participate. It might also be a sort of blueprint for the French New Novel.

A detective novel of Quain's *El Dios del laberinto* (*The God of the Labyrinth*), begins with a mysterious murder and ends with the solution to the crime. However, the solution is followed by a very long paragraph which contains the sentence: "Todos creyeron que el encuentro de los dos jugadores de ajedrez había sido casual" ("Everyone believed that the encounter between the two chess players was the product of chance"). The narrator informs us that this statement allows the reader to understand that the solution presented earlier was erroneous and that consequently the reader re-reads the pertinent chapters and in this way discovers "otra solución, que es la verdadera." (another solution, which is the true one.) The very next words are significant. "El lector de ese libro singular es más perspicaz que el detective" (*Ficciones*, 79). ("The reader of that singular book is more perspicacious than the detective.")

It is made quite clear: the reader is more perspicacious than the detective. This is essential. The difficulty involved in solving the mystery combined with the conquest of that very same difficulty lends the reader a sense of intelligence, of superiority with respect to the detective, and even with respect to the author of the book; hence the narrator's oxymoronic reference to the Siamese Twin Mystery as "agradables y arduas involuciones" ("pleasant and arduous complications").

It is clear, then, that in spite of the great differences between the two writers, Robbe-Grillet's work exhibits certain affinities with that of Borges. These affinities are not merely thematic, but technical as well. At times a theory or a method is simply mentioned by Borges while it is put into practice by Robbe-Grillet. We have observed that there are indications of a definite motive in Borges for these jumbled scenes, for a detective plot, for the utilization of myths, labyrinths, stories within stories and other examples of internal duplication, for the manipulation of time. The motive is to permit "those imperfect writers, whose name is legion," to take part in the production of the work of fiction. Or, as the narrator of "Examen de la obra de Herbert Quain" says, "the reader, distracted by vanity, thinks he has invented them [the stories]." The novels and films of Robbe-Grillet owe a great deal of their charm to that invitation to the reader/spectator to take part in the literary work.

Robbe-Grillet has praised Borges' work and has referred to it on several occasions. For example:

A writer who could turn out a skillful pastiche, so skillful that he could even produce some pages that Stendhal might have put his name to at the time, would have none of the value that he would still have today if he had written the same pages in the reign of Charles X. It was not a paradox that J. L. Borges propounded in this connection in his *Ficciones*: a twentieth-century novelist who copied *Don Quixote* word for word, would in doing so, be writing a totally different work from that of Cervantes. (*Snapshots...*, 45.)

In addition to revealing a familiarity with Borges' work on Robbe-Grillet's part, this also suggests that the French novelist agrees with the Argentinean writer with reference to the idea of the reader as writer. It would be difficult to demonstrate, at this time, that Borges has had a direct influence on Robbe-Grillet (the chronology makes it impossible for the influence to have proceeded in the opposite direction), in fact, in a conversation with me, Robbe-Grillet denied this influence.[40] Nevertheless, it is undeniable that there exists at least a basis for comparison between the two authors.

Borges' aversion to the genre of the novel is well-known: he reaffirms this position when interviewed by Fernando Sorrentino in 1972:

> No, I never thought of writing novels. I think if I began to write a novel, I would realize that it's nonsensical and that I wouldn't follow through on it. Possibly this is an excuse dreamed up by my laziness. But I think Conrad and Kipling have demonstrated that a short story --not too short, what we could call, using the English term, a 'long short story'-- is able to contain everything a novel contains, with less strain on the reader (*Seven Conversations*, 145.) [41]

Well-known too is his method of pretending that a non-existent book exists in order to write a synopsis or review of that book. Borges has commented on this procedure: "The composition of vast books is a laborious and impoverishing extravagance: one which expounds at length in five hundred pages on an idea the perfect oral exposition of which could be accomplished in a few minutes. A better procedure is to pretend that those books already exist and to offer a summary, a commentary... More sensible, more inept, lazier, I have preferred to write notes on imaginary books" (*Ficciones*, the Prólogo.)[42]

Borges never wrote a novel and prefers the short story; Robbe-Grillet is a novelist. The Argentinean is blind while the Frenchman has an extremely visual orientation. Yet in spite of these superficial differences, on a deeper level there are definite thematic and technical similarities. The devices employed by both writers --labyrinths, manipulation of time, allusions to and reworkings of myths, the detective format, repetition of scenes-- appear to be directed at one goal in the case of both authors: that of obliging the participation of the reader in the work of fiction. This participation, along with the pride of accomplishment it engenders in the reader, could account for one facet of the attraction exerted by the work of the two writers.

WORKS CONSULTED

Borges, Jorge Luis. *Discusión*. Buenos Aires: Emecé, 1964.
_____. *Ficciones*. Buenos Aires: Emecé, 1956.
_____. *Otras inquisiciones*. Buenos Aires: Emecé, 1960.

Robbe-Grillet, Alain. *L'Anée derniere a Marienbad*. Paris: Editions de Minuit, 1961.
_____. *Dans le Labyrinthe*. Paris: Editions de Minuit, 1959.
_____. *Glissements progressifs du plaisir*. Paris: Editions de Minuit, 1973.
_____. *Les Gommes*. Paris: Editions de Minuit, 1953.
_____. *La Jalousie*. Paris: Editions de Minuit, 1957.
_____. *La Maison de rendez-vous*. Paris: Editions de Minuit, 1965.

_____. *La Maison de Rendez-vous*. Trans. Richard Howard. New York: Grove Press, 1966.
_____. *Projets pour une revolution a New York* (1970).
_____. *Snapshots and Toward a New Novel*, trans. Barbara Wright. Lodon: Calder and Boyars, 1965.
_____. *Two Novels by Robbe-Grillet: Jealousy & In the Labyrinth*. Trans. Richard Howard. New York: Grove Press, 1965.
_____. *Le Voyeur*. Paris: Editions de Minuit, 1955.
Sorrentino, Fernando. *Seven Conversations With Jorge Luis Borges*. Trans. Clark M. Zlotchew. Troy, N.Y.: Whitston, 1982.
_____. *Siete conversaciones con Jorge Luis Borges* Buenos Aires: Casa Pardo, 1973.

CHAPTER 6

CARLOS FUENTES' *AURA*:

MAGIC, SEX AND DESTINY

Carlos Fuentes' novella, *Aura*, depicts an iron-clad destiny: Felipe Montero will answer the newspaper want-ad which seems meant for no one but him, will accept the position offered by Consuelo, the elderly mistress of the mysterious old house in downtown Mexico City, will take up residence in that house, will fall madly in love with Aura, the beautiful young girl who, in fact, is nothing but the magical projection of Consuelo's youth, conjured by witchcraft, and will finally become the reincarnation of General Llorente, the long-deceased husband of Consuelo. The plot makes this clear, but the plot is seconded by the symbolic imagery and even by the grammatical structure of the language.

When one reads a novel or short story from the viewpoint of the third person, he or she conceives of the events as happening to someone else, the one referred to by the speaker. When the work is narrated in the first person, these events still happen to someone else: to the person speaking to the reader. However, when the reader is constantly bombarded with the subject pronoun tú, tú, tú (you, you, you), he or she is made to feel that the reader, and not someone else, is experiencing the events narrated. The reader is, in a sense, reading about his or her own adventures, if disbelief is sufficiently suspended for the duration of the reading.

The reader of *Aura* is the protagonist, then, so that when the narrator finally becomes General Llorente, it is the reader --who has been Felipe Montero up to this point-- who changes identity once more. If Montero really is the reincarnation of the General, rather than one who is bewitched into believing so, this change of identity is in reality a return to a former identity, the closing of a circle.

The sense of implacable fate and of a circular movement provided by the language is not limited in cause to the use of the second person singular. Even the grammatical tenses employed contribute to this effect. Whereas the past tenses (imperfect and preterit) and the present tense are the most common tenses used in Spanish-language narrative, in *Aura* Fuentes exclusively utilizes two tenses: the present and the future. In itself the future tense has the effect of emphasizing the inevitability of the reader-narrator's fate (you will do this, this will happen), while the constant shift from present to future to present provides a circularity of movement that imitates and foreshadows the death and reincarnation of General Llorente and the cycle of birth, aging and death of Aura, Consuelo's projection.

Aside from the grammatical structures of the novel, the imagery that Fuentes employs provides a highly symbolic framework for the sense of relentless destiny, witchcraft and eroticism which leaps from the pages of *Aura*. When Felipe Montero is being interviewed by the elderly Consuelo, Aura first makes her appearance. The situation is described as follows:

> --Es el señor Montero. Va a vivir con nosotras.
>
> Te moverás unos pasos para que la luz de las veladoras no te ciegue. La muchacha mantiene los ojos cerrados, las manos cruzadas sobre un muslo: no te mira. Abre los ojos poco a poco, como si temiera los fulgores de la recámara. Al fin, podrás ver esos ojos de mar que fluyen, se hacen espuma, vuelven a la calma verde, vuelven a inflamarse como una ola: tú los ves y te repites que no es cierto, que son unos hermosos ojos verdes idénticos a todos los hermosos ojos verdes que has conocido o podrás conocer. Sin embargo, no te engañas: esos ojos fluyen, se transforman, como si te ofrecieran un paisaje que sólo tú

puedes adivinar y desear.
　　　--Si. Voy a vivir con ustedes. (Fuentes, p. 81).⁴³

　　"This is Mr. Montero. He's going to live with us."
　　You will move a few paces so that the light of the candles does not blind you. The girl keeps her eyes closed, her hands crossed on one thigh: she does not look at you. She opens her eyes little by little, as though she feared the brightness of the bedroom. Finally, you will be able to see those oceanic eyes that flow, turn to foam, once more become a calm green, once more become inflamed like a wave: you see them and you repeat to yourself that it's not true, that they are a pair of beautiful eyes just like all the beautiful green eyes you have ever known or will ever be able to know. Nevertheless, you don't deceive yourself: those eyes do flow, they become transmuted, as though they were offering you a landscape that only you can interpret and desire.
　　"Yes. I'm going to live with you."

This passage is near the beginning of the novel, at the point in which Consuelo tells Felipe --or tells the narrator/reader-- that he will have to live in her house, this dark and decrepit mansion, if he wishes to accept the position as editor of her deceased husband's memoirs. At this point Felipe has not yet made his decision. Aura makes her first appearance here. This beautiful companion of the old woman appears in the darkness of Consuelo's bedroom without Felipe's hearing her approach; she simply appears, as though out of the void. The reason Felipe does not hear Aura approach is that she does not really approach; she suddenly comes into being because she is, as the reader realizes by the end of the novel, the projection of Consuelo's youth, the product of her witchcraft.
　　It appears that her previous form was that of the pet

rabbit which Consuelo keeps in her bed. Consuelo tells Felipe that Saga (the rabbit's name), who has just left the bed and disappeared into the darkness, is "Mi compañía" ("my companion) and that it will return (Fuentes, 80). Several paragraphs later, when Aura makes her silent and sudden appearance, Consuelo tells Felipe, "Le dije que regresaría..." ("I told you [she] would return...") Felipe asks, "¿Quién?" ("Who?") to which the elderly lady replies, "Aura. Mi compañera. Mi sobrina" ("Aura. My companion. My niece") (Ibid. 81).

Rabbits, or hares, are associated in the popular mind with procreation and fecundity. According to Cirlot, "In Greece, the lunar goddess, Hecate, was associated with hares" and "The German equivalent of Hecate, the goddess Harek, was accompanied by hares" (Cirlot, p. 139). Saga, the rabbit, is the witch's familiar and doubles as her projection of Aura, her own youthful self.

Hecate is a "symbol of the Terrible Mother, appearing as the tutelar deity of Medea or as a lamia who devours men. She is a personification of the moon, or of the evil side of the feminine principle, responsible for madness, obsession and lunacy" (Ibid. 143). She also requires human sacrifice (Ibid. 188). In this battery of equivalences between Consuelo, Saga, and Aura, we find a powerful erotic force that will bewitch the protagonist and finally devour him.

When Felipe first sees Aura, her eyes are closed. She opens them very gradually, as though she is not accustomed to the candle light of Consuelo's bedroom. Perhaps this is because Aura, this projection of another's will, has just been "born," so to speak, and is not yet accustomed to the light. Perhaps she has come from a region which is even darker than Consuelo's bedroom.

The highly metaphorical and oceanic language succeeds in making Aura's green eyes reveal the strong emotions of the depths of her soul, i.e. of Consuelo's soul. Water, in general, symbolizes life and, at the same time, paradoxically, death. "Immersion in water signifies a return to the pre-formal state, with a sense of death and annihilation on the one hand, but of rebirth and regeneration on the other, since immersion intensifies the life-force" (Ibid. 365). Baptism, which employs water, represents the death of the former person and life for the new one. Among the ancients, water, like earth, was a female principle (Ibid. 365). According to Cirlot, "water stands as a mediator between life and death, with a two-way positive and negative flow of creation and destruction" (Ibid. 365). Ancient peoples believed that the sun dies each night in the western ocean and is reborn each morning in the eastern ocean, so that the ocean, specifically, became symbolic of life and death, of birth and regeneration. This is one of the themes of *Aura*: time is cyclical, and within these cycles Consuelo-Aura ages, is rejuvenated, ages once more, and is rejuvenated ad infinitum, while General Llorente dies only to be reincarnated. The ocean is, in addition, "a symbol of woman or the mother (in both her benevolent and her terrible aspects)" (Ibid. 242). In *Aura*, the cycles of recurring life and death are brought about by Consuelo, woman as Terrible Mother and witch.

Aura's eyes are not only beautiful and oceanic; they are also green. The color green is endowed with multiple symbolisms in Spanish. As the antonym of the adjective seco ("dry," i.e. "dead") it is applied to plants that retain their sap. Consequently, it stands for life as opposed to death, since the sap of plants corresponds to the blood of animals. The color is identified with the Spring season, the season in which the sap begins to rise in plants and in which trees begin to put forth their leaves, and in which grass begins to grow, clothing fields in green after the winter. In this way, it becomes the color of regeneration and acquires the symbolic values of hope and of the Resurrection.

Nevertheless, the color green has a figurative connotation related to obscenity and lasciviousness, as in the expressions viejo verde ("green old man," i.e. "dirty old man") and chiste verde ("green joke," i.e. "dirty joke"). For viejo verde, the Dictionary of the Royal Spanish Academy of the Language includes this definition: "Dícese del que conserva inclinaciones galantes impropias de su edad o de su estado" ("Said of one who retains amorous inclinations unbefitting his age or position"). While this symbolism may seem far removed from those involving hope and the Resurrection, these seemingly contradictory meanings share a common denominator. The viejo verde is one who, in spite of his chronological age, still retains --or believes he retains-- the vital juices of his youth; he hopes to put them to good use.

The color green, then, symbolizes generation and re-generation. It is an erotic color in Spanish symbolism because it is related to the season of mating and to reproduction. It stands for life, the reproduction of life, and rebirth of life.

Vernon B. Chamberlin has noted that at least as late as 1886 in Spain, the audience of a play still responded to the symbolism of the color green, even without actually having to see the color on the stage. Chamberlin also reports that the great Spanish writer Benito Pérez Galdós, at the peak of his realistic phase, continued to use erotic green as a symbol (Chamberlin, pp. 31, 33).

In *Aura* there are twenty-two references to the color green associated in some way with Aura or with Consuelo as a young woman. Most of the references are to Aura's eyes (Fuentes, 81, 85, 99, 105, 106), or to young Consuelo's eyes (Ibid. 94, 95, 106), or to Aura's clothing (Ibid. 83, 91, 97, 99, 102, 107) or to the clothing of young Consuelo (Ibid. 95). In addition, the curtains of Consuelo's mansion are green (Ibid. 77, 83), as is the slime coating the bottles of wine served to Felipe Montero in Consuelo's home (Ibid. 84) and even the toothpaste he uses there (Ibid. 97).

In the above-quoted passage, there are three uses of the adjective verde without counting the implied reference to the color contained in the oceanic metaphors. At the beginning of the passage, Consuelo matter-of-factly states that the protagonist is going to live in that house, although he has not yet said he will. At the end of the passage, one that describes the fascination Aura exerts on Felipe, especially with her green eyes, he definitely agrees that he will be staying with the two women. Consuelo's assurance that Felipe will succumb to her alter ego's attraction, followed by Felipe's agreement, reinforces the growing feeling of inevitability, of destiny, which fills this novel.

At the end of the novel, Felipe Montero enters Consuelo's room in order to take the third packet of papers from the chest kept in a corner of the room:

> Caminas hasta el baúl colocado en el rincón; pisas la cola de una de esas ratas que chilla, se escapa de la opresión de tu suela, corre a dar aviso a las demás ratas cuando tu mano acerca la llave de cobre a la chapa pesada, enmohecida, que rechina cuando introduces la llave... (Ibid. 104).

> You walk up to the chest in the corner; you tread on the tail of one of those rats which squeals, escapes from under the pressure of your sole and runs off to warn all the other rats when your hand brings the copper key to the heavy, rusty, metal lock which creaks as you insert the key...

In traditional Western symbolism, with good reason rats are associated with sickness and death. The frequent presence of these animals in Consuelo's room is consonant with the physical condition of this very old woman who is constantly ill and hovering near death. When Felipe extracts the third bundle of General Llorente's letters from the ancient chest, he hurriedly leaves the room with them, without closing the chest, forgetting, the narrator pointedly tells us, "el hambre de las ratas" ("the rats' hunger") (Ibid. pp. 104-05). The implication is that the rats would devour the memoirs of the General, which would consign him to oblivion, allowing his memory to die. At other points in the novel, the animals in the vicinity of the chest are referred to as "ratones" ("mice") which, in medieval symbolism, are associated with the devil (Cirlot, p. 272).

Consuelo is a witch, and the power of witchcraft has

traditionally been deemed to stem from the devil. According to General Llorente's papers, when he tried to dissuade her from practicing her magic, he indicated that he felt she was opposing God: "Consuelo, no tientes a Dios" ("Consuelo, don't tempt God [to punish you]") (Fuentes, p. 105). He finally suggests that she will be involved with the devil if she persists: "Consuelo, también el demonio fue un ángel, antes" ("Consuelo, the devil was an angel too, before.") (Ibid.).

Cirlot states that a "phallic implication has been superimposed on it [symbolism of mice], but only insofar as it is dangerous or repugnant" (Cirlot, p. 272). The phallic implication could be generalized to a sexual one which is dangerous or repugnant; this would agree with the nightmares in which Felipe has sexual relations with an old woman with toothless, bleeding gums (Fuentes, pp. 92, 96-97).

The insertion of the key into a lock is of transparent sexual significance, but Fuentes reinforces this commonly understood Freudian interpretation by stating that the key is made of copper, a metal traditionally associated with Venus, goddess of love and fertility (Cirlot, p. 209). Jung believes that base metals refer to the desires and lusts of the flesh (Cirlot, p. 208). The chest is mouldy. The lock is rusty and creaks when the key is inserted. The images in this passage foreshadow or suggest the possibility of the protagonist's engaging in sexual intercourse with a woman who in reality is exceedingly old, thus reinforcing the message delivered in Felipe's nightmares.

Although the young Consuelo desired to have children but found she was unable to do so, she finally substitutes for them this projection of her own youth by means of magic arts. Her inability to have children, as well as her placing a spell on Felipe, suggest the figure of the Greek goddess Hecate, archetype of the Terrible Mother who devours men and brings about their obsessions and madness (Cirlot, p. 143). Hecate is also associated, among other things, with keys (Ibid.).

In *Aura*, Carlos Fuentes has produced a literary work in which the very grammatical structure combines with a battery of symbolic images to suggest an inexorable destiny produced by witchcraft and eroticism.

WORKS CONSULTED

Chamberlin, Vernon A. "Symbolic Green: A Time-Honored Characterizing Device in Spanish Literature," *Hispania*, 51 (1968), 29-37.

Cirlot, J. E. *A Dictionary of Symbols.* trans. from Spanish by Jack Sage. Second edition. New York: Philosophical Library, 1971.

Fuentes, Carlos. *Aura.* In *Triple espera: Novelas cortas de Hispanoamérica*, edited by Djelal Kadir. New York: Harcourt Brace Jovanovich, Inc., 1976.

CHAPTER 7
JULIO RICCI: TIME TRANSMUTED INTO SPACE

Much of the fiction of Julio Ricci centers on various types of grotesques who inhabit what Italian critic Meo Zilio refers to as "la plúmbea cotidianeidad montevideana" ("the leaden everydayness of Montevideo") (p. 550). On the other hand, a significantly high proportion of Ricci's short stories concerns characters who originate in Eastern Europe or the Middle East. While a great deal of the Uruguayan writer's fictional world is bathed in an aura of poetry and magic,[44] this poetry and this magic are much more evident in the works that deal with Poles, Russians, Ukranians, Hungarians, Russian and Turkish Jews, and Armenians. These denizens of the Middle East and the territory behind what was the Iron Curtain suffer as much, if not more, than the native Uruguayans, but have a mysteriously noble, spiritual dimension to their lives which is of profound interest to Ricci.[45]

The Uruguayan narrator of "Pivoski" visits an old friend born in Poland. The apartment, in the Old City of Montevideo, is dark, disorderly, filthy, unheated and foul-smelling, yet the narrator has a sense of well-being in this atmosphere because in it he finds human warmth and a sense of intimacy that he has always associated with "la Europa central y... los Balcanes" ("central Europe and the Balkans") (*maniáticos*, p. 11). The narrator is not only more comfortable in this gloomy, stinking pigsty ("pocilga lúgubre y hedionda"), he is actually ecstatic in it because, "dominaba por sobre todo el espíritu del hombre, de ese hombre único e intransferible que era Pivoski" ("what stood out above everything else was the spirit of the man, of that unique, untransferable man who was Pivoski") (Ibid. pp. 11-12). The narrator becomes more effusive, declaring that being in this apartment is equivalent to having arrived in the Promised

Land, the place of his dreams (Ibid. p. 12). His own home is well-lighted, neat, clean and warm, yet the narrator feels that something is missing from his modern, technologically perfect dwelling. In Pivoski's decrepit flat he immediately recovers his happiness and feels like a new man (Ibid.).

An element originating in a different region of Ricci's enchanted geography is introduced and associated with Pivoski: the Turkish coffee to which the Pole had become accustomed when living in Istanbul for three years before settling in Montevideo. At this point, the narrator insists on his enchantment in the presence of Pivoski (Ibid. p. 13). The atmosphere of the flat is summed up with two cases of oxymoron: "En un ambiente tan acariciadoramente lúgubre, en una atmósfera tan íntimamente sórdida... ("In such a caressingly gloomy ambience, in such an intimately <u>sordid</u> atmosphere...") (My emphasis, Ibid. p. 18). This juxtaposition of negative adjectives and positive adverbs links the dark and gloomy surroundings paradoxically to feelings of affection, intimacy and well-being.

The Uruguayan narrator of "La carta" ("The Letter"), Juan González, writes a letter to a Polish woman he had met at the Warsaw airport and with whom he had conversed on the flight from the Polish capital to Copenhagen ten years earlier (*Cuentos*).[46] The narrator considers this woman to be extraordinary precisely because she is Polish.[47] Yet, in his initial references to his nostalgia for places visited in the past, Turkey is involved once more: "Una boleta de cambio de dinero en Estambul, por ejemplo, desencadena en mi mente decenas de vivencias. Vuelvo al Gran Bazar, cruzo el Cuerno de Oro en un barco, me veo de nuevo en un café de La Calle Galata o de la Plaza Taksim" ("A chit for currency exchange in Istanbul, for example, triggers dozens of personal experiences [in my mind]. I'm back in the Great Bazaar, I'm crossing the Golden Horn on a ferry, I see myself once more in a café on Galata Street or in Taksim Square") (*Cuentos*, p. 126; *Falling*, p. 32). Other items he has saved bring him back to Warsaw and then to Bucharest. As in "Pivoski," in which there is a bridge --the Balkans-- joining Poland to

Turkey, in "La carta" the same axis --Poland, Rumania, Turkey-- unites the territories of Ricci's enchanted region.

González, following in the footsteps of the narrator of "Pivoski," experiences physical discomfort --including, once more, a cup of unappetizing coffee-- while being charmed by his companion's humanity. The bitter coffee, the stale cake, the numbing cold of the unheated airliner, are more than compensated by Iwona's warm personality. In "La carta," as in "Pivoski," humanity is preferred to the technological advances of a world which Is becoming less human every day: "Entre tanta máquina el contacto humano tal vez sea como una luz en las tinieblas, una ventana a la vida" ("Surrounded by so many machines, human contact might be a sort of light in the gloom, a window on life") (*Cuentos*, p. 129; *Falling*, p. 34). Alone in his apartment in Montevideo, having returned from his soul-deadening, routine-filled desk job, the narrator states and then repeats that he is happy just thinking of his conversation with Iwona ten years earlier.

González associates the city of Warsaw with Iwona. His initial impressions of the city had been of intense cold, people hiding inside their houses, hiding inside their souls, a massive black building dominating the city, and Iwona, clad in black. This negative image proves to be false; he finds that the inhabitants of the Polish capital have a zest for life as well as a desire to help the stranger.[48] As in Pivoski's apartment, the physical surroundings contrast with the traits of the human spirit.

Iwona has about her something "de bohemia, de vencida, de decadente" ("bohemian, defeated, dispirited") (Ibid.). Her clothing is old and worn. The narrator is pleased that she has not attained two qualities he associates with fine new clothing: "importancia" ("[self-]importance") and "desfachatez" ("impudence") (Ibid.). This Polish woman is associated, as was Pivoski, with odors that Westerners attempt to avoid. This is a positive factor for González because it indicates that Iwona is not a member of the consumer society which dominates the West: "Hasta tenía el olor de los no muy favorecidos. El consumismo no la había invadido de plano. No estaba tocada por olores artificiales" ("You [Iwona] even had about you the smell of those not favored by fortune. You were not subject to the consumer society and were untouched by artificial odors") (Ibid. 129-30). This lack of artificiality confers upon Iwona a secular odor of sanctity.

It is revealing that in thinking of Warsaw, González refers three times in one short paragraph to oldness ("vetusta" ['ancient' or 'decrepit']; "viejo" ['old']; "reliquia" ['relic']), while he romanticizes Iwona's links with the past into myth and poetry: "Tal vez Ud. [Iwona] había emergido de las aguas grises, de la espesa niebla del Vístula, de algún poema polaco" (Perhaps you [Iwona] had emerged from the grey waters, from the thick fog of the Vistula, from some Polish poem") (Ibid. p. 130). It is significant that the narrator's leaving Poland prevents him from saying something beautiful, intimate, to Iwona because, "la atmósfera diferente de Dinamarca, los seres mecánicos del aeropuerto, rompieron el encanto" ("the different atmosphere of Denmark, the machine-like beings at the airport, broke the spell") (Ibid. p. 131). The spell of ancient, poetic Poland is broken in contact with the modernized, prosaic West in which the narrator is greeted by robot-like airport employees. He is once more plunged into the sea of incommunication which Ricci believes typifies our advanced Western civilization, and is inhibited from functioning on a personal, human level.

"El Shoijet" is the story of an elderly Uruguayan gentleman, Pedro López, who sets out to find his childhood friend, Lázaro Dorón, a Russian-born Jew.[49] The narrator deeply admires, even idealizes, the Jewish people. In much the same way that the Polish woman of "La carta" was not an ordinary woman, in "El shoijet" the narrator declares that his friend "no era un muchacho como los demás" ("was not a boy like the others") (*Grongo*, p. 22). This is true not only because of Lázaro's intelligence and good character, but because of his exotic origins and the air of mystery which the narrator feels surrounds Lázaro: within this short story there are eleven instances of the use either of the noun "misterio" ("mystery") or the adjective "misterioso" ("mysterious") with reference to Lázaro, to other individual Jews, or to the Jewish people (Ibid. pp. 22, 29, 24, 26, 27). The concept is further heightened by the employment of eight other terms conceptually related to the aforementioned noun and adjective.[50]

The attribution to the Jews of secrets, incomprehensible mystery and magic had for centuries instilled fear and loathing of this people in the hearts of Christians.[51] For thousands of years Jews have been accused of murdering Christian children for ritual purposes.[52] Yet these mysterious qualities, for the Uruguayan narrator of "El shoijet," even as a child, are positive factors. Pedro López even begins to study the Hebrew tongue with his playmate in order to gain entry into the fascinating world of the Children of Israel (G, p. 22). A glance at the lexicon demonstrates that this is because young López sees their magic as good rather than evil. This goodness is insisted upon as though it were a leitmotif; some form of the adjective bueno (good) is utilized eight times in this short story with reference to the Jews (G, pp. 23, 26, 28, 29, 30, 31, 32). If related adjectives are added to this figure, there are eleven references to the goodness of this people.[53] In the mind of the narrator of "El shoijet," a surrogate for Ricci himself,[54] the prime qualities of the Jews are magical mystery combined with moral excellence; the descendants of the ancient Israelites are practitioners of good magic.

They possess other qualities, too. Unlike Ricci's Poles, his Jews are surrounded by material comforts; at any rate, this is the narrator's impression on visiting the shops of the Jewish quarter of Buenos Aires. He sees piles of merchandise, brightly colored fabrics, people energetically moving packages from one place to another, and he smells delightful fragrances. He imagines that behind all this mercantile activity sits "algún anciano hebreo contando dinero o abstraído en meditaciones misteriosas, en esas meditaciones que yo buscaba ahora comprender pero que se me escapaban" ("some venerable Hebrew sage counting coins or lost in mysterious meditations, in those meditations I was then trying to comprehend but which kept evading me") (*Grongo*, pp. 26-27; *Falling*, 67). In the narrator's mind still lurks the ancient stereotype of the Jew counting money as well as engaged in magic or religious meditations.[55] Nevertheless, the context in which the old stereotype is found is positive: López wishes to be a part of this attractive world. Ironically, on observing this perennially persecuted and beleaguered people, the narrator declares, "¡Qué feliz y qué segura era esa vida entre paquetes y colores y perfumes y mercaderías!" ("How happy and secure was that life among packages and colors and perfumes and merchandise!") (*Grongo*, p. 27; *Falling*, 67).

In his spellbound observation of the Jewish shops, López experiences the sensation of travelling in time, returning to the ancient world, to the bazaars of Asia filled with "maravillas y misterios infinitos" ("infinite marvels and mysteries") (*Grongo*, p. 27; *Falling*, p. 67).). He thinks the Jews know how to live like lords among opulent surroundings because "venian del Asia" ("they came from the East") and "eran hombres de *Las mil y una noches*" ("were men straight out of *The Thousand and One Nights*") who know and control the great secrets of existence. At this point, López feels envy (Ibid.; Ibid.).

As in Pivoski's squalid flat, in which the atmosphere was different from that of most of Montevideo, Lázaro's home contains "una atmósfera distinta" ("a different atmosphere") (*Grongo*, p. 23). The specific atmosphere associated with the People of the Book is one of spirituality, of the sacred.[56] The narrator's contemplation of the synagogues of Montevideo leaves him in a state of ecstasy (*Grongo*, p. 25; *Falling*, 65). Ecstasy is also the state experienced by the narrator of "Pivoski" while in the Pole's apartment (*maniáticos*, p. 11).

In the Jewish hotel of Buenos Aires, the narrator encounters great human warmth and homey friendship among the elderly men who gather in the lobby each evening to chat. He is so comfortable among these people --who more than half the time speak Yiddish, a language unintelligible to López-- that he, like Odysseus among the lotus-eaters, temporarily forgets his mission in the Argentine capital: to seek out his childhood friend, Lázaro Dorón. The reason for the lapse is that "Es inimaginable lo bien que me sentía alli" ("You can't imagine how comfortable I felt there") (Grongo, p. 25; *Falling*, p. 65). The Jews of "El shoijet" represent a materially comfortable world balanced by deep spirituality as well as human warmth, magic and moral rectitude. These qualities are highly prized by the narrator.

A different kind of Jew is the protagonist of "Historia de una radio" ("The Story of a Radio") (*Ocho modelos*). José Niño is not a Yiddish-speaking native of Russia; he is a Spanish-speaking native of Turkey, a descendant of the Jews expelled from Spain in Columbus' time. This Sephardi is neither mysterious nor particularly spiritual; in fact, Niño differs very little from the ordinary Uruguayans who populate the short stories of Ricci, except that he, unlike the native-born Uruguayans, lives miserably in the present in order to safeguard his old age.[57]

José Niño is a good man, but an ordinary man. The reason he possesses none of the mystery or spirituality found in the Jews of "El shoijet" must lie precisely in his ordinariness, in his lack of exoticism. His speaking a dialect of Spanish even before settling in Uruguay allows him to blend into local life much more readily than the Jew who speaks an outlandish Germanic tongue. Furthermore, Niño is from Izmir, a city on the Aegean (Mediterranean) coast of Turkey with a climate similar to that of Montevideo or, for that matter, to the Mediterranean ports of Spain and Italy, countries from which the ancestors of the average Uruguayan have come. It is only the Ashkenazic Jew --proceeding from villages like those of Marc Chagall's luminous fantasies, villages situated on the frozen, windswept steppes of Poland and Russia-- whom Ricci views as fascinatingly different, as mysterious and spiritual.

In "El shoijet," the ancient Hebrew language was, for the narrator, the key to the unknown. Significantly, the single point at which the mundane story of José Niño and the coveted shortwave radio takes on some of the mysticism that pervades "El shoijet" is at the very end, during the funeral services for the protagonist, and in close relationship with the Hebrew language and religion. The officiating rabbi chants prayers In the Holy Tongue, and then speaks of Niño's life, of friendship, the mysteries of human existence and the hereafter. Then, as Niño's friends --Christians and Jews alike-- participate in filling the grave with earth, the Uruguayan narrator is inspired to compose several lines of poetry regarding the brevity of human life (*Ocho*, p. 82). The rabbi speaks once more, and the cemetery takes on a dreamlike quality for the narrator. At this point, precisely as happened to the narrator of "El shoijet" while peering into the Jewish shop windows, the narrator feels as though he were transported in time and in space, to "la antigüedad" ("ancient times") and to "el Asia Menor" ("Asia Minor") (Ibid.). The rabbi then intones Hebrew prayers which, for the narrator, are deeply moving, are "palabras mágicas" ("magic words") even though --or perhaps because-- he does not understand them.

The visions of the people who originate in Eastern Europe and in the Middle East afforded by Ricci's short stories are at times contradictory. There is opulence and there is squalor. There is physical comfort and there is material discomfort. There are delightful fragrances and foul odors. Nevertheless, there are also qualities held in common. The characters emanating from these eastern lands are invariably associated in some way with what is old, whether ancient or merely old-fashioned. The values of this world are also ancient or old-fashioned: moral rectitude, spirituality, human warmth, intimate friendship and love. Around this core of values Ricci casts a numinous glow of mystery and magic.

Exoticism in fiction tends to be the expression of a

writer's dissatisfaction with the world in which he lives. The writer finds his surroundings too painful to bear, and seeks escape in dreaming of other times or of other climes. Ricci's narrators try to escape the mechanized, computerized, dehumanized Western world of today by entering an older, more human world. Because Pivoski's apartment and Iwona's Warsaw are uncomfortable and malodorous --the way the West was a century ago-- Ricci feels it also retains the human spiritual qualities he believes were once found in the West. At the same time, the Jewish religion and the Hebrew language, associated with the Holy Bible, suggest to Ricci the mysteries of the origin of life and the ancient moral values which he feels are swiftly disappearing.

While Ricci's dissatisfaction with the modern West can be deduced simply by a reading of his works of fiction, these deductions are supported explicitly in speaking directly with him. Answering a query about the tango, which bore no obvious relation to his fiction, Ricci said:

> En la gran época del tango (los años 40 y 50, años de mi juventud)... [el] hombre estaba más apegado a la familia, había menos movilidad social, menos máquinas.... Estaba [el hombre] más arraigado al barrio.... Estaba incluso más ligado sentimentalmente a los amigos.... (Zlotchew, *El hombre fracturado*, p. 133; Zlotchew, *El inmovilismo*, p. 127).

> During the grand epoch of the tango (the 40s and 50s, the years of my youth)... a man was more attached to his family. There was less social mobility, fewer machines... He [man] was more deeply rooted in his neighborhood... He was even emotionally closer to his friends... (Zlotchew, *Voices*, p. 90).

Whereas the past represents a period in which the absence of social mobility and the absence of a high degree of mechanization are equated with greater social cohesion and deeper friendship, life in the modern world is "como una eterna partida de ajedrez de un nivel de stress incalculable" ("like an eternal chess game at an incalculable level of stress") (Zlotchew, "Entrevista" p. 82; Zlotchew, *Voices*, p. 84). Merely surviving in any of the large cities requires "una salud mental enorme" ("an enormous amount of mental health"), because "[t]odo es lucha por la vida. Todo es ajustarse a nuevas situaciones, y eso coloca al hombre en un estado de inquietud y de desequilibrio (*Discurso.*, p. 83) ("The struggle for life is all. All is adjusting to new situations, and this places man in a sate of turmoil and disequilibrium") (*Voices*, p. 84). That he refers specifically to the Western world is explicit: "El avance cada vez mayor del psicólogo en Occidente muestra la situación de inseguridad y caos de las masas... en este inexplicable Occidente de hoy (Ibid. pp. 83-84). ("The constantly growing importance of the psychologist in the Western World shows a situation of insecurity and chaos among the masses... in our unfathomable West of today") (*Voices*, p. 85).

For many, one means of escape from the rigors of the workaday world is through poetry, for others it is religion, spirituality or contemplation. Ricci's definition of poetry is revealing; it is, he says:

> ...una esencia, un algo misterioso e indefinible que produce un estado muy especial o un rapto inexplicable en el alma y que tal vez corresponde a la captación de algo inefable, de algo que no podemos explicar claramente, pero que nos acerca de algún modo a lo que sería el secreto de la vida, de la creación, del tiempo (Zlotchew, "Europa, p. 134).
>
> ...an essence, a certain mysterious, indefinable something [that produces a very special state or an inexplicable rapture] in one's soul which perhaps corresponds to the grasping of something ineffable, of something we cannot make explicit with any clarity, but which, in some way, brings us closer to what might be the secret of life, of creation, of love, of time. (*Voices*, p. 88).[58]

The elements of this Riccian definition of poetry -- metaphysical concepts that others associate with spiritual, even mystical, pursuits-- are those sought by the narrators of the stories dealing with the regions and characters of a swath of territory extending from Russia and Poland through the Balkans to Turkey and the Middle East. This magical territory is Ricci's refuge from the dystopia of the impersonal, technologically advanced modern world: Ricci's modern West. It represents his escape into the poetry of a world which is still as human, and as magical, as he imagines the West of his youth was. Unable to travel in time, Ricci's narrators (and through them, Ricci himself) travel in space and magically transmute time --the golden age of the author's youth-- into space: a utopian geographical region to the East and Southeast of Europe.

WORKS CONSULTED

Aínsa, Fernando. *Tiempo reconquistado*. Montevideo: Ediciones Géminis, 1978.

"Blood Libel." *Dateline: World Jewry*. June 1990, p. 7.

Graetz, Heinrich. *History of the Jews*, trans. from German. Philadelphia: The Jewish Publication Society of America, 1898.

Johnson, Paul. *A History of the Jews*. New York: Harper & Row, 1987.

Kalechofsky, Robert and Roberta, general editors, *Echad: An Anthology of Latin American Jewish Writings* (Marblehead: Micah Publications, 1980)

Mann, Thomas. *Death In Venice and Seven Other Stories*, trans. by H. T. Lowe-Porter, Vintage Books, a Division of Random House. New York: Alfred A. Knopf, 1936.

Margolis, Max L. and Alexander Marx. *A History of the Jewish People*. Philadelphia: The Jewish Publication Society of America, 1927.

Mathews, Tom. "The Long Shadow." *Newsweek* 115.19 (7 mayo 1990): 43.

"Medieval 'Blood Libel' Canard Promoted by an Italian Church." *Response: The Wiesenthal Center World Report*, 10.2 (September 1989): 1-2.

Meo Zilio, Giovanni. "El neorrealismo de Julio Ricci, entre onirismo y gestualidad: Apuntes estilísticos," *Revista Iberoamericana*, 49, 123-124 (April-September 1983).

"Minneapolis Blood Libel." *Response: The Wiesenthal Center World Report*, 11.2 (May 1990): 15.

Ricci, Julio. *Cuentos civilizados* (Montevideo: Ediciones Géminis, 1985).

_____. *Falling Through the Cracks: Stories of Julio Ricci*, trans. Clark M. Zlotchew. Buffalo: White Pine Press, 1989.

_____. *El Grongo*. Montevideo: Ediciones Géminis, 1976

_____. Letter to Clark M. Zlotchew, July 6, 1985.

_____. "The Letter," trans. Zlotchew, *Webster Review*, 10, 2 (Fall 1985), 40-46.

_____. *Los maniáticos*. Montevideo: Editorial Alfa, 1970.

_____. *Ocho modelos de felicidad*. Buenos Aires: Macondo Ediciones, 1980.

Samuel, Maurice. *Blood Accusation: The Strange History of the Beilis Case*. New York: Alfred A. Knopf, 1964.

Sorrentino, *En defensa propia* (Buenos Aires: Belgrano, 1982).
_____. "In Self Defense," trans. Zlotchew, *Webster Review*, 9 I (Spring 1984), 87-83.
Zlotchew, Clark M. "Entrevista con Julio Ricci," *Discurso Literario: Revista de Temas Hispánicos*, 5, 1 (1987), 75-86.
_____. "Europa en la ficción del uruguayo Julio Ricci," in *El hombre fracturado en la narrativa de Julio Ricci: Siete estudios críticos* (Paris & Montevideo: Signos, 1990), pp. 125-38.
_____. "Desde el Infierno al Paraíso: la búsqueda en Julio Ricci," in *El inmovilismo existencial en la narrativa de Julio Ricci*. ed. Isolde J. Jordan. Montevideo: Editorial Graffiti, 1993, 123-142.
_____. *Voices of the River Plate: Interviews With Writers of Argentina and Uruguay*. San Benardino: Borgo Press, 1995.

CHAPTER 8
JULIO RICCI: RETURN TO EDEN

When reading Julio Ricci's short story, "El shoijet" ("Old Friends"),[59] one receives the unmistakable impression that something profound lies beneath the simple plot concerning an old man who attempts to find his childhood friend. The reader experiences the sensation that something transcendent is stirring beneath the surface, surreptitiously driving the entire narrative. It is difficult to describe this sensation or to isolate the reasons for experiencing it, but it is undeniably present. We feel as though we were in the presence of the mythic or of material originating in the author's unconscious, and which speaks directly to our own. In order to be able to analyze this short story in a meaningful way, it is important first to examine certain aspects of Ricci's work in general.

From his first book of short stories, *Los maniáticos* (1970), passing through *El Grongo* (1976), *Ocho modelos de felicidad* (1980), *Cuentos civilizados* (1985), *Los mareados* (1987), and *Cuentos de fe y esperanza* (1990), up to his last collection, *Los perseverantes* (1993), this Uruguayan short-story writer has observed the effects on the life of the individual human being caused by urban life in the Western World. Ricci's narrations --impregnated with a sense of humor at times open and good-natured, at times bitter and black-- emphasize the struggle for survival of the ordinary person in the Big City, as well as the diminution of human beings faced with the preeminence of the very machines created by them.

We observe a world that is highly computerized and bureaucratized --dehumanized-- through which the individual squirms in spiritual isolation from his/her fellows. We feel pity for these lonely and humble people. We also stumble upon possibilities for communication, for understanding, for friendship and love --for hope-- scattered here and there in the mud of a debased, depressing landscape.

Certain concerns appear in Ricci's very first stories which remain constant throughout his literary trajectory. Loneliness is one of them. We find antiheroes like the man who, having been ejected from his house by the wife who no longer loves him, spends all his time at the corner bar in order to spy on the house that had been his home, thus voyeuristically feeling himself to be part of the family. Then there is the timid young man who lives on dreams and daydreams. Fearful of rejection, he never gets up the courage to speak to the attractive young woman who waits for the bus every day at the same street corner. Instead, he spends his waking life looking forward to the night, when he retires to his canopied bed to dream of her. The years pass and Juancito dies alone.

"El apartamento" ("The Apartment") is the story, in very realistic surroundings, of a man so alone, so lonely --in a European city, far from his native Montevideo-- that he falls in love with a chair to which he gives the name María (G). As an example of Ricci's tongue-in-cheek humor, the narrator solemnly complains that "era triste que un objeto y un ser humano que se quisieran no pudieran unirse en el supremo y unificador hechizo del amor" ("it was sad that an object and a human being in love with each other could not unite in the supreme and unifying enchantment of love") (G, 90).

In Ricci's first three books, we observe the loneliness of those who live in the Big City, ironically in physical contact with so many of their fellows, but isolated from them in spirit. This loneliness, which is accompanied by lovelessness and alienation, is precisely what leads to the grotesque behavior of so many Riccian characters. This loneliness and lack of communication continue to be present in Ricci's fourth book, *Cuentos civilizados*, but this time in combination with other themes which had been present --not as a central theme, but as a corollary-- in Ricci's previous books. In this collection the concept of routine and the problems of bureaucracy are accentuated to the point of being on a par with the theme of loneliness.

In *Cuentos civilizados* the author leads us along an extension of the paths established in 1970, but these paths now traverse a thicker, darker, gloomier, more dangerous forest than that of fifteen years earlier. The absurd is still present, but expressed with more bitterness, more force and less humor. The Riccian universe has always resembled the darkly absurd and bureaucratic world of Franz Kafka, an author greatly admired by Ricci, [60] but in these "civilized" short stories the bureaucracy is even more arbitrary, and human beings are more dehumanized --which is not synonymous with "less human"-- than their Kafkaesque counterparts. This is not a coincidence; Kafka, living in a Europe that still retained vestiges of nineteenth-century civilization, was prophesying, was glimpsing the future. Ricci, on the other hand, wrote in the midst of our genocidal nuclear age, a time of social disintegration and chronic distrust.

Routine now also attains a place of great importance in Ricci's narrative. Furthermore, the author's attitude toward routine is ambivalent. The narrator of "La carta" ("The Letter") detests the routine of his life: "La rutina, la odiosa rutina... La gente de la oficina está siempre como enferma por eso. Porque repiten día tras día lo mismo" ("Routine, odious routine... The people at the office are always sort of sick because of it. Because day after day the repeat the same thing") (CC, 126). Routine is powerful: "Con los años, el hábito es tan fuerte que cualquier cambio es trágico. No poder tomar el té a las 4 es una especie de cataclismo para el hombre-rutina" ("With the years, habit becomes so strong that any change is tragic. Not being able to have tea at 4 o'clock is a kind of cataclysm for routine-man") (Ibid. 127). But if he hates routine, it is only because missing from the routine of his are friendship and love: "Vuelvo presuroso de la rutina a mi apartamento y hago todo rápido para poder sentarme y hablar con Ud. [en la imaginación]" ("I rush back from my routine to my apartment and I get everything done fast in order to sit down and speak with you [in my imagination]") (Ibid. 129). The reader cannot help but wonder what the narrator's routine would be like if it included the woman he loves. The problem, for the narrator of "La carta," is that his routine is a routine of loneliness.

Through almost all the stories of *Cuentos civilizados*, but more obviously, more centrally, in "La pared," "La jerarquía," "El gerente," and "La baba," there runs the theme of bureaucratic rank. In these stories, the strict logic of the bureaucracies is raised to the dizzying heights of a modus vivendi that destroys the peace of mind of the office workers and even of the executives themselves.

The manner in which the individual's destiny depends on the inscrutable arbitrariness of the quasi divine Directorio (Board of Directors) of the commercial enterprise reflects real life, but is exaggerated, magnified to absurd lengths in Ricci. Riccian hyperbole lends the all-powerful Directorio (also referred to as the "Superioridad" [literally, the "Superiority"] in "La pared"), takes on universal, metaphysical, cosmic dimensions that are reminiscent of Jorge Luis Borges' "La lotería en Babilonia" ("The Lottery in Babylon") and, at the same time, because of the gratuitous suffering occasioned, the biblical Book of Job.[61]

Ricci's stories are not pretty. They oblige us to see what perhaps we might prefer to ignore. Many of his narratives are aggressive, ugly and hyperbolic. Nevertheless, there is a streak of fantasy and idealism in them because, as Ricci says through the narrator of "La carta," "para todo lo importante en la vida se necesita trascender la realidad" ("for everything important in life one must go beyond reality") (Ibid. 131). This concept is essential to understanding a certain slant within Ricci's writings.

Although part of Julio Ricci's fiction concentrates on the various types of grotesques inhabiting what Meo Zilio has designated "la plúmbea cotidianeidad montevideana" ("the leaden daily life of Montevideo") (Meo Zilio, 550), a good many of Ricci's stories deal with characters born in Eastern Europe or the Middle East. And although Ricci's narratives, in general, lay bare a vision "empapada de poesía y magia" ("permeated with poetry and magic") (Ainsa, 185), this poetry and this magic manifests itself much more clearly in the works in which the most important characters are Poles, Russians, Ukrainians, Hungarians, Russian Jews, Turkish Jews and Armenians. These natives of the Middle East and of the vast territory that lies behind what was once the Iron Curtain, suffer as much as the native Uruguayans, but they also possess a mysteriously noble and spiritual dimension that fascinates Ricci.[62]

The Easterner of Eastern Europe and of the Middle East is, naturally, exotic for the "Easterner" of the República Oriental del Uruguay, the official name of Uruguay, referring to its position on the eastern bank of the Uruguay River. The various kinds of ambience that form the background of the stories dealing with these exotic characters are contradictory. There is opulence and there is squalor. Physical comfort and tangible discomfort are both present. We find delightful fragrances as well as evil odors. Still, all these milieus have one quality in common: The characters proceeding from these lands invariably are associated with what in one way or another is old, ranging from truly ancient to merely old-fashioned. The values of this world also are either ancient or old-fashioned: moral rectitude, spirituality, human warmth, deep friendship and love. Around this nucleus of values Ricci wraps the radiance of mystery.[63]

One might wonder what Ricci's exoticism signifies. Exoticism in fiction tends to be the expression of the writer's dissatisfaction with the world in which h/she lives. The author finds that his/her surroundings are too painful to bear, and attempts to escape from them by dreaming of other times and other climes. Ricci's narrators endeavor to flee the mechanized, computerized, dehumanized world of today's West, in order to enter a world that is older, more human, more humane. This is why the tiny apartment of a Polish immigrant ("Pivoski") and the Warsaw of "La carta," described as uncomfortable and even gloomy --as was the West a century ago-- captivate Ricci's characters who feel that these environments still retain those human and spiritual qualities now lacking in their own lives. At the same time, the Jewish religion and the Hebrew language --both associated with the Bible-- suggest to Ricci's mind the mysteries of the origin of life and the ancient moral values which he believes are rapidly disappearing.[64]

While it is true that one deduces Ricci's dissatisfaction with the modern Western world simply by reading his works of fiction, this deduction is supported by Ricci himself in direct conversation. In answering a question that had no obvious relation to his work, Ricci responded:

> En la gran época del tango [los años 40 y 50, años de mi juventud]... El hombre estaba más apegado a la familia, había menos facilidades materiales, menos movilidad social, menos máquinas... Estaba [el hombre] más arraigado al barrio. Estaba incluso más ligado sentimentalmente a los amigos... (Zlotchew, "Utopian Escapism...," 150).

> During the grand epoch of the tango [the forties and fifties, the years of my youth]... A man was more attached to his family. There were fewer material conveniences, fewer machines, less social mobility... A man was more deeply rooted in his neighborhood... He was emotionally closer to his friends... (Zlotchew, *Voices...*, p. 90).

While the past represents an era in which the absence of social mobility and the lack of a high degree of mechanization are equated with greater social cohesion and deeper friendship, life in the modern world is "como una eterna partida de ajedrez de un nivel de stress incalculable" (Zlotchew, "Entrevista...", 82) ("Life is like an eternal chess game at an incalculable level of stress.' [Zlotchew, *Voices...*, p. 84). Merely surviving in any of the great cities requires "una salud mental enorme" ("an enormous amount of mental health"), because "Todo es lucha por la vida. Todo es ajustarse a nuevas situaciones, y eso coloca al hombre en un estado de inquietud y de desequilibrio" ("Entrevista...", 83) ("The struggle for life is all. All is adjusting to new situations, and this places man in a state of turmoil and disequilibrium") (*Voices...*, p. 84).

That Ricci refers specifically to the Western world is explicit: "El avance cada vez mayor del psicólogo en Occidente muestra la situación de inseguridad y caos de las masas" ("Entrevista...," 83) ("The constantly growing importance of the psychologist in the Western World shows a situation of insecurity and chaos among the masses" *(Voices...,* 85). Ricci insists on the geography: "...en ese inexplicable Occidente de hoy" ("Entrevista...," 84) ("...in our unfathomable West of today") (*Voices...*, 85).

For many, poetry represents a means of escape from the daily struggle for survival in a hard and prosaic world. Ricci's definition of poetry is revealing:

> ...una esencia, un algo misterioso e indefinible en el alma y que tal vez corresponde a la captación de algo inefable, de algo que no podemos explicitar claramente, pero que nos acerca de algún modo a lo que sería el secreto de la vida, de la creación, del amor, del tiempo (Ricci's letter to Zlotchew of 6-6-85).
> ...an essence, a certain mysterious, indefinable something in one's soul which perhaps corresponds to the grasping of something ineffable, of something we cannot make explicit with any clarity, but which, in some way, brings us closer to what might be the secret of life, of creation, of love, of time (Zlotchew, "Utopian Escapism...," 151, and *Voices...*, 88).

The elements of this Ricciesque definition of poetry are the very same ones sought after by the narrators of the stories dealing with the regions and characters of Ricci's East: the territory that extends from Russia and Poland, passing through the Balkan countries to Turkey and the Middle East. This magic space is Ricci's refuge from the dystopia of the technically advanced but impersonal modern world: the West. It is his vision of a world that still --at least in Ricci's imagination-- remains as human, as magical, as he imagines the West of his childhood was. Unable to travel in time, Ricci's narrators travel through geography, transmuting a specific era --the golden age of the author's childhood-- into space: the utopian geographical region located to the east and southeast of central Europe.[65]

We have seen that the Ricciesque definition of poetry involve terms such as essence, mysterious, indefinable, soul, ineffable, secret of life, of creation, of love, of time. These are concepts usually associated with religion o, more precisely, with religious experiences, with mysticism. What Ricci provides as a definition of poetry would be, for others, the definition of a mystical or religious experience: the voice of God. For still others, perhaps it would be a definition of the Freudian id or the Jungian collective unconscious. After all, Freudians and Jungians, despite the great divergences that exist between their respective approaches to the study of the human psyche, tend to explain religious experiences in psychological terms.

The point is that what for some can be interpreted in religious or mystical terms, and for others can be explained "scientifically" (but psychoanalysis could easily represent yet another religion), for Ricci represents poetry. Or at least, poetry is the term he prefers to employ. Nevertheless, the definition does not change that which is defined. A rose by any other name would still be a rose. Ricci's theory of poetics, the qualities his fictional characters seek, what for Ricci appears to be concealed in those magical "eastern" regions, what, in the final balance, Ricci himself longs to discover is precisely:

> "...an essence, a certain mysterious, indefinable something in one's soul which perhaps corresponds to the grasping of something ineffable, of something we cannot make explicit with any clarity, but which, in some way, brings us closer to what might be the secret of life, of creation, of love, of time."

In his works of fiction Ricci leads us into that hell in which subsist the outcasts and other grotesques created by his imagination but based on his observation of daily reality. But these characters yearn for something better. The personages of the "eastern" narratives (e.g. "Pivoski"; "La carta" ["The Letter"; "El shoijet" ["Old Friends"]) actively seek that better something, reflecting the deepest yearnings of Ricci himself. And that something better happens to coincide with the above-quoted Ricciesque definition of poetry. That is to say, in this author's fiction we certainly encounter a Dantesque *Inferno*, but we also glimpse, if we read carefully, the *Paradiso* longed for and sought after by Ricci's characters and by the author himself.

All of which brings us back to the first paragraph of this study, to the short story, "El shoijet" ("Old Friends"). This narration brings us closer than any other of Ricci's stories to the Ricciesque definition of poetry. "Old Friends" is nothing less than the quest for Paradise, in religious terms, the quest for the mystical experience, for communion with God. Or, in Jungian language, the pursuit of individuation, the uniting of the unconscious with consciousness, the union of opposites in order to obtain the wholeness of the ego. It is the mythical quest. In any event, it is the Quest, with a capital Q.

"Old Friends," translated into English twice,[66] on the most superficial level deals with an elderly non-Jewish Uruguayan, Pedro López, who undertakes a search for his childhood friend, Lázaro Dorón, a Russian-born Jew. López feels that Lázaro was different from the other boys (G, 22). This is so not only because of his intelligence and highly moral character, but also because of his exotic origins and the mystery that the narrator believes surrounds the boy. Within this very short story there are eleven cases of the use of the noun misterio ("mystery") or the adjective misterioso ("mysterious") with reference to Lázaro, to other Jewish individuals, or to the Jewish people (G, 22, 23, 24, 26, 27). This concept is augmented by the utilization of eight other terms conceptually related to mystery.[67]

It is this mystery, these secrets, that fascinate the narrator, that makes him wish to enter that special world: "Mi mente de niño aún bullía de curiosidad. Deseaba desentrañar los secretos de ese mundo europeo que él sin proponérselo representaba y que se ocultaba en sus gestos, en sus miradas y hasta en sus sonrisas, que yo hallaba misteriosas y a veces inexplicables" ("My childish mind still seethed with curiosity. I wanted to unravel the secrets of that European world which he unintentionally represented and which was concealed in his gestures, in his glances and even in his smiles, which I found mysterious and at times inexplicable") (G, 22).

Seeking entrance into this world, López asks Lázaro to teach him Yiddish, the language in which Lázaro communicates with his parents. But Lázaro tells him that if he wants to learn an important language, he should study Hebrew. After learning several phrases in Hebrew within a few months, López feels "transportado" ("carried away' or 'ecstatic' or 'enraptured") with joy when using this language with Lázaro (G, 23). Feeling "transportado" goes beyond merely feeling content. For the narrator, the Hebrew language is the secret key to the mysteries of life.

The attribution to the Jews of secrets, incomprehensible mystery and magic had for centuries instilled fear and loathing of this people in the hearts of Christians. For thousands of years Jews have been suspected of murdering Christian children for ritual purposes.[68] In many quarters this suspicion subsist even today. [69] Yet these mysterious qualities, for the Uruguayan narrator of "El shoijet," even as a child, are positive factors. Pedro López even begins to study the Hebrew tongue with his playmate in order to gain entry into the fascinating world of the Children of Israel (G, p. 22).

A glance at the lexicon demonstrates that this is because young López sees their magic as good rather than evil. This goodness is insisted upon as though it were a leitmotif; some form of the adjective bueno (good) is utilized eight times in this short story with reference to the Jews (G, pp. 23, 26, 28, 29, 30, 31, 32). If related adjectives are added to this figure, there are eleven references to the goodness of this people.[70] In the mind of the narrator of "El shoijet," a surrogate for Ricci himself,[71] the prime qualities of the Jews are magical mystery combined with moral excellence.

The atmosphere the narrator associates with the Jewish people is spiritual, sacred. Lázaro's grandfather, a rabbi, gives the appearance of one who has come from some temple or "lugar sagrado" ("holy place") in which serenity, respect and austerity reign, as well as "grandeza de espíritu y el amor por todo lo desconocido" (G, 23) ("greatness of spirit and love for all that is unknown" [*Falling...*, 63]). The synagogues López visits in his search for Lázaro contain an impressive austerity and seriousness, and the Ark that contains the Torah (the sacred scroll of the Five Books of Moses, Deuteronomy) possesses a simple nobility and a grandeur that for López is "indescriptible" ("indescribable") (G, 25). We are in the presence of the ineffable. The narrator would become ecstatic ("me extasiaba") while gazing at the interior of the synagogues of Montevideo. Ecstasy, it should be remembered, is an experience intimately associated with mysticism, specifically at the moment of the soul's union with God.[72]

Having been unable to locate Lázaro in Montevideo, López thinks his old friend might have relocated across the river to Buenos Aires. He flies there. In a hotel in the Jewish quarter of Buenos Aires, the narrator feels a deep human warmth and close friendship among the elderly men who gather in the lobby every evening for chitchat. He is so comfortable among these people --who usually speak Yiddish, a language unintelligible to López-- that he, like Odysseus among the lotus eaters, temporarily forgets his mission in the Argentine capital: to search for his boyhood friend, Lázaro Dorón. The reason for this lapse, according to the narrator, is that "Es imaginable lo bien que me sentía allí" (G, 25) ("You can't imagine how comfortable I felt there" [*Falling...*, 65).

This hotel represents for Ricci the era of his own youth, the grand epoch of the tango about which he is so nostalgic, an era in which, according to Ricci, man was "more deeply rooted in his neighborhood... ...emotionally closer to his friends..." (*Voices...*, p. 90). The Jews of "Old Friends," then, represent not only mystery and high morals, but also human warmth which for Ricci has disappeared from the modern West.

In "Old Friends" there is a great deal of movement through physical space. The narrator is so desirous of finding his childhood friend that he visits every synagogue in Montevideo and speaks with every rabbi. When he cannot locate Lázaro anywhere in Montevideo, he flies to Buenos Aires, where he stays at the Jewish hotel. Finally he pulls himself away from that comfortable circle of human warmth, that "calorcito" ("cozy warmth"), to continue his quest (G, 26). Every day he visits the shops of the Jewish district in which the mere names of the stores remind him of cities dreamed of in his imagination, enchanted lands, "cosas extrañas" ("strange things") (G, 26). On looking through the store windows he becomes highly emotional: "Toda mi alma se volcaba en la contemplación" ("My entire soul turned over as I gazed") (G, 27).

López does not find Lázaro in Buenos Aires, but does find him later in Montevideo, on moving to another apartment. It is important to note that he finds him only after undertaking those trips, that long quest in which he crossed and recrossed the wide estuary called the Río de la Plata (the River Plate). Significantly, Joseph L. Henderson, the prestigious Jungian psychologist, sees in the symbol of the solitary journey or pilgrimage one of the most common oneiric symbols that represent liberation from a state felt to be too final (Jung, *Man...*, 149-52). This symbol indicates the need, according to Henderson, for freeing oneself from a form of existence felt to be unsatisfying in order to move to a higher level of psychic development (Ibid.).

Furthermore, Henderson explains that although a child feels psychically whole, this is so only before the awareness of the Self makes its appearance. Adults, on the other hand, achieve a feeling of wholeness only when able to unite the conscious mind with the contents of the unconscious. According to Jung, from this union (the transcendent function of the psyche) a person can reach his/her most important goal, that of the full realization of the potential of his/her individual Self (Ibid. 149). What Jungian psychologists designate "symbols of transcendence" are the symbols that represent man's struggle to reach that goal. These symbols are found in myths and history as well as in the dreams of modern people who are at a crucial point in their lives.

Thinking of Ricci's "Old Friends" it is significant that according to Henderson one of the most apt symbols of psychic transcendence is the image of the bird. The bird image is one form of the Trickster figure, but not in its most common form: the self-styled licentious hero. The Trickster has been converted into the shaman or sorcerer whose magic practices and flights of intuition mark him as the primitive master of the initiation process. His power resides in his supposed ability to leave his body and fly around the universe in the form of a bird (Ibid. 151).

According to Henderson, both the symbolism of the bird and that of the solitary journey, the pilgrimage, represent the desire to unite the conscious mind with the unconscious, to free one's mental powers and thus fully realize the potential of one's individual Self. As stated above, these symbols arise in an individual when he/she feels the need to move to a higher mental plane.[73] In order to search for Lázaro Dorón, Pedro López, the narrator of "Old Friends," undertakes what unhesitatingly could be called a solitary journey. Even the term "pilgrimage" would not be inexact, in view of our above analysis of the lexicon of this short story.

This pilgrimage is carried out on both shores of the River Plate, in the synagogues and Jewish neighborhoods of Montevideo, and in the shops and the hotel of the Buenos Aires "ghetto." Furthermore, part of the voyage involves air travel; the airplane is the modern counterpart of the bird, symbol of liberation, of the transformation of the psyche. The narrator flies. Within the pages of this brief narration, then, we find both the pilgrimage symbol and the bird symbol.

The presence of these synonymous symbols in "Old Friends" provides a powerful double-barreled presentation of the concept of the liberation of mental powers. These symbols insist on the struggle to move from one psychic level to a higher one. Following this line of reasoning, it is remarkable that according to M.-L. von Franz, crossing a river is a symbolic image, frequently encountered in dreams, of a fundamental change of mental attitude on the part of the dreamer (Ibid. 199). Crossing that broad estuary known as the River Plate, then, expresses subconsciously, but unequivocally and powerfully, the desire for liberation from certain life habits in order to ascend to a different plane of existence, fulfilling the potential of the Self in so doing.

All this agrees with what Pedro López expresses in the first paragraph of "Old Friends": "Ya hacía años que tenía esta costumbre de sentarme y rememorar, de querer reconstruir el pasado, de buscar en él algo que no encontraba en el presente y que seguramente no me traería el futuro" (G, 21) ("I'd been doing that for years: sitting down and thinking of the old days, wanting to reconstruct the past, searching for something in that past that I couldn't find in the present, and that I surely was not going to find in the future") (*Falling...*, 61).

The narrator demonstrates great dissatisfaction with his life; something is lacking in it. This is why he goes off in quest of his boyhood friend. Of course, it is possible to say simply that López is nostalgic for his youth and that Lázaro represents that youth. This conclusion has validity, but does not go far enough, since López's quest, as he well knows, will not bring back his youth. Besides, when he does find Lázaro --now an old man, of course-- López inexplicably cannot bring himself to identify himself to his old friend. Clearly, this quest represents an internal journey, and Lázaro Dorón --Lázaro Dorón as a child-- is the unconscious symbol of the goal of this quest.

The integrated Self (the ego combined with the id, the conscious mind with the unconscious) often appears in myths and in the dreams of men in the symbolic form of the archetype of the Wise Old Man; it also appears as the Young Man (Jung, 196) [74] Von Franz reports that these apparently paradoxical personifications attempt to express something that is not contained entirely within time, something that is timeless, that is simultaneously young and is old (Ibid.). If this concept appears in the form of the Young Man, then the symbol emphasizes a renewal of life, the Self renewed, a creative élan vital, and a new spiritual orientation by means of which everything becomes filled with life and the spirit of enterprise (Ibid. 199). This is what the figure of Lázaro Dorón symbolizes in Pedro López's mind. This is the true goal of his quest.

Lázaro Dorón, the child Lázaro, however, is more than that; this figure contains a double charge, and is therefore a powerful image. Not only is Lázaro the personification of the Self in its renewing aspect, but at the same time is the representation of the half of something very important that must be (re)united with the other half.

The integration of conscious elements with unconscious material (Jung's individuation) also appears symbolically as the union of opposites. These opposites take a variety of forms, many of which are found represented in the symbolism of various religions and world mythology as well as in art. For example, the design of the yantras, the Buddhist and Hindu figures utilized in meditative exercises, are purely geometrical.

According to Aniela Jaffe, a very common yantra is formed by two interpenetrating triangles, the tip of one pointing upward, the tip of the other downward. This symbol is identical to the Hebrew Seal of Solomon or Shield of David which dominates the scene in the funeral home at the end of "Old Friends": "En el fondo, dos sencillos candelabros y la estrella de Sión que dominaba el ambiente" (G, 33). "In the back of the room were two simple candelabra and the Star of David dominating the scene" (*Falling...*, 73).

Jaffe states that traditionally this design symbolizes the union of Shiva and Shakti, the masculine and femenine Hindu deities (Jung, 240). The psychological symbolism of this yantra --and of all the manifold artistic-symbolic representations of the union of male and female-- expresses the union of the opposites. The psychological opposites are the personal, temporal, conscious world as juxtaposed to the impersonal, atemporal, unconscious world. Jaffe maintains that this union is the fulfillment and the goal of all religions: the union of the soul with God (Ibid.).

This union of the opposites can take on an almost infinite number of forms. It could consist of the union of the color white with the color black, or of the small with the large, ad infinitum. In Benito Pérez Galdós's novel *Gloria*, the sexual union between Gloria, a Catholic woman, and Daniel, a Jewish man, results in the birth of Jesús, whose destiny is to unite the "enemigas razas" ("enemy races"), and who, according to the narrator of *Gloria*, is the "personificación más hermosa de la Humanidad emancipada de los antagonismos religiosos por virtud del amor" ("most beautiful personification of Humanity emancipated from religious antagonisms by virtue of love") (Galdós, 682). Similarly, the Christian and the Jew of "Old Friends," the native-born Uruguayan and the foreigner, are opposites. Pedro López, spokesman for the author himself, expresses what Julio Ricci feels.[75]

The voyage Pedro López undertakes in search of Lázaro Dorón represents the desire --the need-- of the author to unite the opposites, the conscious and unconscious elements of his psyche. By means of this short story, Ricci expresses this longing to free himself from one form of existence --an existence, as we have seen, in world that is mechanized, dehumanized, devoid of human warmth-- in order to move to a higher level of psychological development. This story represents a process of initiation, the passage from one stage of life to another. It is symbolic of the need for a transition in Ricci's life. It is the literary expression of a rite of passage.

At critical moments of life, the archetype of initiation becomes exceedingly active in the psyche in order to bring about a transition that offers a spiritually satisfying experience. The archetypal forms of initiation in this religious sense --known as "the mysteries" in Antiquity-- are interwoven within all ecclesiastical rites that require special ceremonies to mark the moments of birth, marriage and death (Jung, 131). In this context, it is revealing that the friendship between Pedro López and Lázaro Dorón is interrupted immediately after an initiation ceremony, of rite of passage:

> Una mañana que casi no recuerdo, los Dorón se fueron del barrio. Se fueron y en mi memoria hay todavía un vacío que no consigo llenar. Lo que sí recuerdo es que pocos días antes de mudarse, los padres le dieron a Lázaro una gran fiesta. Fue una fiesta íntima, una fiesta que a mí me pareció <u>secreta</u> y <u>misteriosa</u>, y que incluso tenía un nombre, un nombre que me sonaba a mágico: Bar Mitzbah. Él me explicó algo. Me dijo que desde ese día sus padres lo consideraban un hombre hecho y derecho y allí terminó todo. Y se excusó por no haberme invitado (My emphasis, G, 24).

> One morning that I can hardly remember, the Dorón's moved out of the neighborhood. They moved away, and there is still a void in my memory that I have not succeeded in filling. What I do remember is that a few days before moving, Lázaro's parents had this grand celebration for him. It was a family affair, a party that to me seemed <u>secret</u> and <u>mysterious</u>, and that even had a special name, a name that sounded magical to me: Bar Mitzvah. He explained a little about it to me. He told that from that day on his parents considered him a full-fledged man, and he said he was sorry he hadn't invited me

(My emphasis on <u>secret</u> and <u>mysterious</u>, *Falling...*, 63-64).

Jung observed that a recurrent theme in neuroses is the loss of a vital sense of the meaning of life, and that an element in the cure of neuroses is the rebirth of that vital sense. The patient must experience an important change by means of the reintegration into the Self of instinctive elements previously separated from the conscious mind. (Ulanov, 112). Anne Belford Ulanov adds that modern man is seeking both his soul and his separated instinctive senses. (Ibid. 112-13). This is precisely what is happening to Pedro López. And to Julio Ricci.

As a whole Ricci's work consists of pictures of alienation. Slochower writes that our era is alienated and alienating. This is due not only to the dislocations of our socioeconomic system, to the hunger for bread. There is a deeper hunger that is not being satisfied: the hunger for self-realization, for being faithful to oneself, the hunger to create. (Slochower, 12). "Today," Slochower adds, "the individual, particularly the creative artist, the writer and the scientist, feel as though in prison, the prison of impersonal authorities" (Ibid. 16). He states that there is a withering of the hope that technical advances with an accompanying increase in material wealth and leisure time would bring joy to the spirit. He points out that many people feel that these technical advances and this material wealth itself tend to increase our spiritual and emotional tensions (Ibid. 13).

Some individuals react to this situation by passively withdrawing from society while others succumb to rage. According to Slochower there is an alternative. Technology lacks a vision of the values created in the past by our living mythic tradition. Identification with the symbolic values of our mythical heroes, as they appear in the outstanding classical works of literature, can counteract the dismal view of the modern world (Ibid. 13-14). The "imitation," in modern literature, of mythical heroes --mythopoesis-- provides us with hope for a rebirth of creativity (Ibid. 17).

In all cases of mythopoesis there a structural unity that consists in the analogous stages of development of mythopoetic heroes from Job to Thomas Mann's Joseph and Sartre's Orestes: these cases always begin when the hero undertakes the Quest. This Quest, the Journey, is the central element of the mythopoetic drama (Ibid. 22). The narrator of "Old Friends" is the mythopoetic hero who takes this voyage of discovery.

Many mythologies describe an initial state of bliss, a perfect world, in which human beings once existed. In this supposed original state, variously called the Garden of Eden, Paradise, the Blessed Isles, Elysium or the Golden Age, man was happy and at peace with nature and his social group. In mythopoesis this state no longer exists, but is only a nostalgic "memory" (Ibid. 23). Pedro López's first words are, "No sé por qué, pero es el caso que poco antes de cumplir los 70 años empecé a pensar y más que pensar a hurgar afanoso en los días de mi infancia y mi primera juventud" (G, 21). ("I don't know why, but just before my seventieth birthday I began to think about --no, it was more than that-- to burrow feverishly into my childhood and early adolescence.") (*Falling...*, 61). The reader wonders why this is so. At the end of the first paragraph we find that the narrator wants to "reconstruir el pasado, ...buscar en él algo que no encontraba en el presente y que seguramente no me traería el futuro" (G, 21). "reconstruct the past, searching for something in that past that I couldn't find in the present, and that I surely was not going to find in the future" (*Falling...*, 61). This is the archetypal nostalgic yearning for the Golden Age, for the original state of bliss. Impelled by this nostalgia, the narrator of "Old Friends," a mythopoetic hero, sets out on his quest. Like Don Quixote de la Mancha, like Krishna, Zoroaster, Osiris, Baldur, Adonis, Bacchus, Hercules, Ulysses, et alia.

Ricci's work taken as a whole presents us with the hellish side of the modern world, but at the same time allows us glimpses here and there of a few heroes who try to steal the sacred fire from the gods, as did the mythical Prometheus. In the short story "El shoijet" ("Old Friends"), this mythopoesis is more obvious than in any other work of Ricci's production. Pedro López seeks entry into the world of magic, of mystery, of the secrets of life and creation, in which he imagines Lázaro Dorón to be living. This is why he undertakes his quest, a quest as mythic as that of Jason's search for the Golden Fleece. Pedro López's quest is the exteriorization, the symbolic representation, of Julio Ricci's subconscious desire to defect from the crass, the empty and the sterile in our mechanized, computerized, dehumanized world.

But Ricci sees the world as sterile and dehumanized because of some emptiness within himself. "El shoijet" ("Old Friends") represents the author's aspiration to satisfy his deeply felt spiritual need to unite his unconscious drives with his conscious mind in one integrated Self, to achieve individuation, to release spiritual and emotional tensions, to re-energize his creative powers. In short, to return to Eden.

WORKS CONSULTED

Ainsa, Fernando. *Tiempo reconquistado*. Montevideo: Ediciones Géminis, 1978.
"Blood Libel" *Dateline World Jewry*. June 1990, 7.
Del Río, Ángel. *Historia de la literatura española*, edición revisada. Volume I. New York: Holt Rinehart and Winston, 1948, 1963.
Graetz, Heinrich. *History of the Jews*, translated from German. Philadelphia: The Jewish Publication Society of America, 1898.
Johnson, Paul. *A History of the Jews*. New York: Harper & Row, 1987.
Jung, Carl G. and M.-L. von Franz, Joseph L. Henderson, Jolande Jacobi and Aniela Jaffe. *Man and His Symbols*. Garden City (N.Y.): Doubleday & Co., 1964.
Kalechovsky, Robert & Roberta, gen. editors. *Echad: An Anthology of Latin American Jewish Writings*. Marblehead: Micah Publications, 1980.
Margolis, Max L. and Alexander Marx. *A History of the Jewish People*. Philadelphia: The Jewish Publication Society of America, 1927.
Mathews, Tom. "The Long Shadow" *Newsweek*, 115, 19 (May 1990): 43.
"Medieval 'Blood Libel' Canard Promoted by an Italian Church" *Response*, 10.2 (September 1989): 1-2.
Meo Zilio, Giovanni. "El neorrealismo de Julio Ricci, entre onirismo y gestualidad: Apuntes estilísticos" *Revista Iberoamericana*, 49, 123-24 (April-September 1983): 547-561.
"Minneapolis Blood Libel" *Response*, 11.2 (May 1990): 15.
Pérez Galdós, Benito. *Obras completas*. Vol. IV. Madrid: Aguilar, 1966.
Ricci, Julio. *Cuentos de fe y esperanza*. Montevideo: Signos y Amauta, 1990.
_____. *Cuentos civilizados*. Montevideo: Ediciones Géminis, 1985.
_____. *Falling Through the Cracks: Stories of Julio Ricci*. trans. C.M. Zlotchew. Buffalo: White Pine Press, 1989.
_____. *El Grongo*. Montevideo: Ediciones géminis, 1976.
_____. Letter addressed to Zlotchew, June 6, 1985.
_____. "The Loser" trans. C.M. Zlotchew. *New Orleans Review*, 16.4 (Winter 1989): 89-97.

_____. *Los maniáticos*. Montevideo: Editorial Alfa, 1970.
_____. *Los mareados*. Montevideo: Monte Sexto, 1987.
_____. "Mr. Szomogy's Best Friend" trans. C.M. Zlotchew. *Webster Review*, 11.2 (Fall 1986): 35-39.
_____. *Ocho modelos de felicidad*. Buenos Aires: Macondo Ediciones, 1980.
Samuel, Maurice. *Blood Accusation: The Strange History of the Beilis Case*. New York: Alfred A. Knopf, 1964.
Slochower, Harry. *Mythopoesis: Mythic Patterns in the Literary Classics*. Detroit: Wayne State University Press, 1970.
Ulanov, Anne Belford. *The Feminine in Jungian Psyuchology and in Christian Theology*. Evanston (IL): Northwestern University Press, 1971.
Zlotchew, Clark M. "Entrevista con Julio Ricci" *Discurso Literario: Revista de Temas Hispánicos*, 5.1 (Fall 1987): 81.
_____. "Europa en la ficción del uruguayo Julio Ricci" in *El hombre fracturado en la narrativa de Julio Ricci: Siete estudios críticos*. Paris and Montevideo: Signos, 1990. pp. 125-38.
_____. "Galdós y los arquetipos" *Letras de Buenos Aires*, año 6, No. 17 (August 1987): 9-14.
_____. *Libido into Literature: The "Primera Época" of Benito Pérez Galdós*. San Bernardino: Borgo Press, 1993.
_____. "Utopian Escapism in Julio Ricci: Golden Age Transmuted into Geography" *Inti: Revista de Literatura Hispánica*, 24-25 (Fall1986/Spring 1987): 145-54.
_____. *Voices of the River Plate: Interviews With Writers of Argentina and Uruguay*. San Bernardino: Borgo Press, 1995.

CHAPTER 9

ANTONIO BRAILOVSKY:

BENEATH THE SURFACE OF REALITY

Antonio Elio Brailovsky, born December 17, 1946 in Buenos Aires, is a complex personality. He has earned his living as a journalist, as a political economist, as a civil servant for the Municipality of Buenos Aires and as Professor of Natural Resources of Argentina at the University of Buenos Aires. In 1990 he was appointed Professor at the Belgrano University. He is also a historian, an ecologist, and has published books of fiction and non-fiction.

His first novel, *Identidad* (*Identity*), published in 1980 by Sudamericana, was awarded First Prize in that year's novel category by the Coca Cola Company's Argentine branch. One of his recent novels, *Esta maldita lujuria* (*This Cursed Lasciviousness*) (Havana: Casa de las Américas, 1992) was awarded the Casa de las Américas Prize. Both the first novel and the last-mentioned one are filled with magic realism. Curiously, both novels deal with the period of Spanish discovery and conquest of the Americas.

Esta maldita lujuria is a hallucinatory picture of the New World as seen through the eyes of a highly suggestible, imaginative, unsophisticated Spanish colonist. This man also relates the stories of sea monsters and Amazons told to him by others. For the sake of relative brevity, this study will concentrate on the writing of *Identidad* and on Brailovsky's concept of magic realism.

Identidad deals with a group of crypto-Jews who, some time after 1492, set out, ostensibly like Cortés, Pizarro and all the other Spanish conquistadores, to conquer and settle territory in the New World. Once at sea, they openly revert to Judaism, change their assumed Christian-Spanish names back to their original Israelite ones, and ban the use of the Spanish language in favor of Hebrew. Like Cortés, they destroy their ship upon reaching land; however, unlike Cortés, they do this in order not to be discovered by the Spaniards. They form a Jewish kingdom in the most inaccessible reaches of the Mexican jungle, after conquering the natives and converting them to Judaism.

These elements of the novel are intertwined with those that deal with the twentieth-century descendants of the conquerors and the conquered: Hebrew-speaking Indians of the Jewish faith who live in villages deep in the jungle. These Jewish Indians fervently await the Messiah who will lead them to the Promised Land. Some have fought at the side of Emiliano Zapata, during the Mexican Revolution, thinking he was the Anointed One. By our own day, some of them desert the villages to follow a Mexican politician whom they believe to be the Redeemer, while others leave to see the wonders of Mexico City and still others join Mexican illegal immigrants on the trip to the Promised Land of California. One group is brought to Israel where they are mistakenly believed to be part of a hoax on the part of a politician.

Identidad plays with time. The fifteenth or sixteenth-century plot progresses in a parallel line with the twentieth-century plot in a series of flashbacks --or flashforths, if the colonization period is taken as the base. The novel --in which characters see their own souls reflected in the eyes of another, and can read the future or the past in those eyes, in which words and ideas materialize into solid objects, and in which the modern Jewish Indians communicate with the ghosts of their ancestors while the founder of the fifteenth-century kingdom can see his twentieth-century descendants-- overflows with magic realism.

Still in Spain, a young boy has not yet been told that they are to take ship to the Indies, but glimpses the future in his father's eyes:

> Manuel Fernando miraba el candelabro ubicado en el centro de la mesa y el reflejo de las velas

en los ojos de su padre, cuya sombre se agigantaba contra el techo. (p. 99).

> Manuel Fernando stared at the candelabrum situated in the center of the table and at the reflection of the candle which began to resemble sails in the eyes of his father, whose shadow loomed immense against the ceiling.[76]

Aside from the fact that the reflection of a candle flame in someone's eyes could certainly resemble a ship's sail, it should be noted that the Spanish word for candle is the same as the word for sail; both are vela. This makes it even more plausible that the vision of the candle flame reflected in his father's eyes should resemble a ship's sails. Still, the metamorphosis works almost as well in English.

The boy contemplates another character:

> Y de tanto comprar y vender esos productos que venían de tan lejos, algo del polvo de la Gran Muralla y del oro de Cipango se habían pegado a los ojos de Simón Benveniste, asomándose a los cuales quizás pudieran verse escenas de naufragios y batallas, y largas caravanas atravesando desiertos de arena. (p. 41).

> And from so much buying and selling of those products that came from so far away, some of the dust from the Great Wall and some of the gold of Cipango had lodged in Simón Benveniste's eyes; perhaps scenes of shipwrecks and battles and long caravans traversing sandy deserts could be seen if one looked into those eyes.

Perhaps, out of the various techniques Brailovsky employs in creating his brand of magic realism, one of the most common ones is the presentation of ordinary events -- with all their objective details to make them vividly real--

filtered through the subjective perceptions, the imagination, of his characters. One example:

> In this way a period of time passed which he was not then able to measure and which afterward no longer mattered, but which he conceptualized as one single immense day, composed of infinite fragments of thirsty marches on horseback beneath a low flat sky in which several simultaneous suns shone against a background of intense blue, almost black, like the open eyes of those who had fallen in battle, eyes that kept drinking it all in back there, forgotten by the troops who continued their interminable march, on that one colossal day on which they had been born on that plain, affixed to their horses forever. (pp. 119-20). [77]

Another example:

> "Yo no vi el mar --les dijo el cacique--, pero le oí el aliento. Es un animal grande, todo de agua. Está aprisionado por las llanuras de los filisteos y lucha por soltarse. (p. 233).

> "I didn't see the ocean," the Chief told them, "but I heard its breathing. It's a large animal, all made of water. It's imprisoned by the plains of the Philistines and is struggling to free itself."

It is not always easy to reach consensus on whether a particular literary work belongs to the magic realism genre, or, more accurately, whether a specific work contains elements of magic realism. Brailovsky's personal ideas on the subject are instructive. Asked to address the difference between magic realism and fantasy, Brailovsky commented: "I believe that reality generally is more fantastic than fiction. That is, we are accustomed to seeing one part, a minor part, of reality. But if we are capable of perceiving reality completely, as a whole, then we find ourselves among things much more extreme than magic." (Zlotchew, *Voices*, p. 61). [78]

While this statement includes a variant of the simple English maxim that truth is stranger than fiction, Brailovsky goes further. Wittingly or not, he is paraphrasing (and translating into Spanish) Shakespeare's "There are more things in heaven and earth, Horatio,/Than are dreamt of in your philosophy." (*Hamlet*), I, v, 166.)

Shakespeare's succinct reference to a magic dimension of reality is repeated and amplified by a twentieth-century writer: "Now, my suspicion is that the universe is not only queerer than we suppose, but queerer than we can suppose... I suspect that there are more things in heaven and earth than are dreamed of, in any philosophy. That is the reason why I have no philosophy myself, and must be my excuse for dreaming."[79]

The idea that truth is stranger than fiction, were the whole truth perceived, lies at the core of magic realism. My own feeling, however, is that magic realism can also stem from a highly subjective observation of the real world. Put another way, it is perceived reality filtered through the imagination, or reality undergoing interpretation.

This process is observable in an example Brailovsky provides of his own brand of magic within realism. He speaks of a short story he wrote for the Argentine magazine *Minotauro*. The magazine had requested a story of either fantasy or science-fiction, but Brailovsky submitted a "rigorously historical story, fanatically documented," on the siege of ancient Syracuse by the Romans. This Greek colony on the island of Sicily was defended by Archimedes, whose secret weapon was the use of parabolic mirrors which employed the sun's rays to set fire to the Roman vessels. This is historical fact.

Brailovsky relates that in the first paragraph of his story we sense the surprise on the part of the Romans. On describing the situation they claim that the Syracusans are "setting fire to the air" around them and burning their ships. "This had to have happened, and happened more or less in this way, according to the eye-witness testimonies of that war," comments Brailovsky. From this, he gathers that magic realism in some way discovers aspects of reality that we have not seen and are not disposed to believe. In fantasy one merely "makes things up." For him magic realism discovers "improbable shades of reality" and is "an opening up of reality" (Zlotchew, *Voices*, p. 61).

Asked about the purpose magic realism serves in fiction, Brailovsky responds that it "enriches the panorama" and "fills it with nuances which otherwise would not appear." He believes magic realism gives fiction a complexity and a subtlety that is not visible when the point of departure is the "grey, ordinary world" of daily life (Ibid.).

While magic realism fairly spills off the pages of Identidad and *Esta maldita lujuria*, there have been moments in Brailovsky's own life which seem like examples of magic realism in a fictional account. If truth is stranger than fiction, and if magic realism is the perception of this magic within our reality, then this is not surprising.

The inspiration for Brailovsky's writing of *Identidad* was a series of imagined visual images so strong that they formed what might be called hallucinations (Ibid. p. 54). The first thing he sensed was a perception of actual scenes. The first scene was that with which *Identidad* opened: a procession of barefoot penitents, following a hooded man dressed in black, whipping themselves and each other, burning incense, dragging huge crosses throughout the length and breadth of Spain at the time of King Ferdinand and Queen Isabella, first co-monarchs of the joint kingdom of Aragón and Castile.

Brailovsky asserts that he very vividly "experienced" the image of the hooded man in black, who announced certain imminent death for all creatures, trailed by the procession described above (Ibid.). He has an explanation for experiencing these near-hallucinatory experiences and the altered state of consciousness which produced them.

In 1975 Brailovsky was a financial reporter for the newspaper *El Cronista Comercial* of Buenos Aires. A wave of violence had begun to sweep the country, and several journalists had been murdered. There were many factions struggling for dominance, and the pressures exerted on the press were, "in the form of bullets". Killing a journalist was the usual method of applying pressure to the editor of a newspaper with the aim of making him modify his editorial line on specific subjects (Ibid.).

At that time a film short appeared on television in which threats were made against the newspapers *La Opinión* and *El Cronista Comercial*. The following day a reporter working for *La Opinión* was murdered, and Brailovsky and his colleagues "were just waiting around for one of us to be killed" (Ibid.). This is when he realized the kinds of degradation fear could produce. He provides an example: He witnessed a group of newspapermen in a huddle, discussing who was most likely to be assassinated next and for what reason. They decided that they didn't have to be overly frightened because the next victims were going to be others. "Still and all," he adds, "not one of us slept in his own house for many days" (Ibid.).

Living in these unnerving circumstances, he found himself seated in a hospital corridor on the evening of May 9, 1974. Beyond one of the closed doors his wife was in labor with their first child. Brailovsky thought about that child who was about to come into the chaotic and frightening world that was Argentina at that time, into a nation that was tearing itself apart, and in which "a man's life was worth much less than some words printed in today's newspaper and which tomorrow would be forgotten" (Ibid.).

It was exactly at that moment that he not only "saw," but actually "felt" the images of the hooded figure in black leading the penitents. It was at that precise moment that he asked the nurse for a pencil and paper and began to write a description of the procession. "Just because I saw it," he says. "I saw the people carrying crosses and flagellating each other in the middle of that hospital hallway" (Ibid.).

In Brailovsky's mind there is a strong connection between the Spanish Inquisition and the situation he lived through in Argentina (Ibid. pp. 54-55). There were torture chambers in his modern Argentina just as there were in the dungeons of the Spanish Inquisition.

One reason for placing this horror at such a great distance in time (five centuries earlier) and space (eight-thousand miles away) was Brailovsky's desire to delve into the origins of the mental set that could lead to the almost daily cases of kidnapping, torture and murder in twentieth-century Argentina. He began to trace these events and this mentality starting with the history of Argentina, but ended by going back to the pre-history of Argentina, i.e. the history of Spain and the rest of Europe.

In this way he began to come up with common denominators, elements present-day Argentina had in common with Medieval Europe and with the Spain of the fifteenth through the nineteenth centuries. One of those elements was the Inquisition. Brailovsky believes that this institution is a factor which has exerted a very strong influence on the daily life of Spain and of the Viceroyalty of the River Plate [under the Spanish Empire, the designation for what was to become Argentina and Uruguay] (Ibid. p. 55).

Although the Inquisition as an institution was abolished in Argentina in 1813, the practices of the Inquisition continued, Brailovsky feels, until 1983, when the Military Junta was replaced by the democratically-elected presidency of Alfonsín. The habits, the mentality, the ideology of the Inquisition still remained. To underscore this, he refers to certain men thought of as philosophers who supported the Military Government and maintained that the struggle was actually not between East and West, not between Capitalism and Communism, as many would have it, but between God and the Devil. What was at stake was the final destiny of humankind. This was the Apocalypse (Ibid. p. 55).

These men felt it was a question of whether humankind would move toward salvation or toward perdition. For them this political struggle was an all-consuming holy war. The battle was between the adherents of God and the worshippers of Satan. This, Brailovsky points out, was absolutely the same ideology found in Medieval Europe, the ideology behind the Inquisition, alive and well in the twentieth century and in the Western Hemisphere. This doctrine was solemnly put into writing by the "philosophers" of the regime. It appeared in books and newspapers and various other forms of print. People who taught at the military schools lectured on it in class (Ibid. p. 55).

Seeing and hearing this apocalyptic vision of the battle between God and the Devil, between good and evil --in which the Military Junta was on the side of the angels while their opponents were with Lucifer-- had a profound effect on Brailovsky. His awareness of this Inquisition mentality right in the middle of modern daily life resulted in his vivid imaginings of scenes that would become the kernel of his novel *Identidad* (Ibid.).

Anyone living in Argentina during the period of the "Dirty War" could not talk about the torture chambers in their own land. Brailovsky realized that if he wanted to describe a torture chamber under the Military Junta, he would have to place it at a distance from Argentina. This, and his desire to trace the Inquisition mentality to its sources, were what Brailovsky consciously thought his reasons were for locating these horrors in fifteenth or sixteenth-century Spain (Ibid. pp. 55-56). He thought he was being very practical.

At a later date he understood that he situated these things as far away as physically possible for deep psychological reasons. He was living through a period of terror, and, "Psychologically, I would not have been able to bear placing it [the horror of the torture chambers] in my own country during that period of time. Even though the censors possibly might have tolerated it" (Ibid. p. 57).

Identidad, Brailovsky's first novel, began with the almost hallucinatory visions its author experienced, visions so uncannily real for him that he felt obliged to write them down immediately. At the same time, Brailovsky so deeply felt the horrors being committed in his own country and in his own time that he found it psychologically indispensable to distance those horrors from himself in time and space.

Keeping these two facts in mind, it would seem that his writing of the novel was a form of catharsis, a way to bring to the surface his deepest fears and, by writing about them, cleanse his psyche of them. He finally became consciously aware of this function of the writing of *Identidad*. When I questioned him about this, he said, "Yes. The description I gave you of how I almost hallucinated the first chapter of my novel *Identidad*... This is catharsis, at least to my way of thinking" (Ibid. p. 62).

Perhaps most illuminating is the magic observable -- to those attuned to it-- in everyday life, in the real world. Brailovsky saw --felt-- the correlation between the mentality of the sixteenth-century Spanish Inquisitors and the mind set of the Argentine Military establishment of his own day. Others might have been aware of this parallel on an intellectual plane, but Brailovsky actually saw and felt the correlation through a kind of waking dream or revelation, his very personal kind of virtual reality.

He experienced the magic dynamically, and was forced to record his impressions on paper in order to rid himself of the anxiety it produced. Brailovsky's sensivity to the magical aspects of reality was the force that prompted the Argentine author to write his first novel, one filled with a luminous aura of magic realism.

WORKS CONSULTED

Bartlett, John. *Familiar Quotations*. Sixteenth Edition. Justin Kaplan, Gen. Editor. Boston, Toronto, London: Little, Brown and Company, 1992.

Brailovsky, Antonio Elio. *Esta maldita lujuria*. Havana, Casa de las Américas, 1994.

_____. *Identidad*. Buenos Aires: Sudamericana, 1980.

Shakespeare, William. *Hamlet*.

Zlotchew, Clark M. *Voices of the River Plate: Interviews With Writers of Argentina and Uruguay*. San Bernardino: Borgo Press, 1995.

CHAPTER 10

ENRIQUE JARAMILLO LEVI:

MAGICAL METAPHORS OF LITERARY CREATIVITY

While the techniques employed by Enrique Jaramillo Levi are eminently recognizable, it might seem difficult, at first glance, to find a common theme in his short stories. His fiction techniques combine the most tangible reality -- whether atrocious or merely crude-- with the most improbable fantasy. Jaramillo Levi combines this realism and this fantasy, adding to them a strong dose of eroticism, in order to create a luminous world in which the magic of the untrammeled imagination reigns supreme. This is clear. However, in order to make generalizations about the thematic aspects of his work, it is necessary first to penetrate the surface and delve deeply.

The longest story of the collection *Ahora que soy él* (*Now That I am He*) bears the deceptively simple title, "El agua" ("Water").[80] This long short story, with its many flashbacks, is the circular delirium --reminiscent of Borges' "El milagro secreto" ("The Secret Miracle") with its story-within-the-story, "Los enemigos" ("The Enemies")-- of a man on the point of committing suicide, a fact the reader is not aware of until the last paragraph of the story. Edwin Pan Kai's motives for suicide are not explicit, but if we search carefully among what might appear to be a chaos of facts and figures on the life and the personal history of this professional magician, we encounter clues.

Some days before the present of this story, Pan Kai notices that in the daily newspapers the same problems and conflicts are constantly being discussed on the editorial page (*Ahora*, 44-45). The narrator refers to the protest demonstrations dispersed by means of night sticks or tear gas in many countries, kidnappings and torture in other countries, and the open violation of the most elemental human rights. Pan Kai sees injustice and pain everywhere and, significantly, he often thinks of how "inútil e insignificante" ("useless and insignificant") he has been, how guilty he is of deceiving people with his tricks instead of educating himself and participating even minimally in some type of fight for justice (Ibid. 45). But he consoles himself with the thought that he is making a good number of people happy, especially children, "que no tenían culpa de nada" ("who were guilty of nothing.") (Ibid.).

There follows a lengthy apology of his art --he is a professional magician. It stimulates children's imagination in a healthy manner, making them forget all the evil in the world. But at the end of this disquisition, he adds, "Lástima que Fanny no le hubiera dado un hijo antes de marcharse" ("It's too bad that Fanny had not given him a son before leaving him.") (Ibid.) In other words, there is an additional reason (the real reason?) for his feeling so "useless and insignificant": Fanny, it turns out, the only love of his life, a passionate love, has left him to go off with another man, after ten years of living with Pan Kai.

Despite having shared those ten years with Fanny, and despite loving children, Pan Kai finds himself growing older without having produced progeny, without having formed a family. This magician has not succeeded in participating in the magic --no less real because of being the most common-- of the reproduction of the human species. Pan Kai finds himself completely alone in the world.

Pan Kai, however, is not a man like all other men. As a child things happened to him that the rest of the world, had it been aware of them, would have called surprising, if not improbable and even grotesque. Once he swallowed two coins, one after the other, and within a short time "las defecó multiplicadas tres veces" ("he defecated them multiplied by three") (Ibid. 37). One of the most fantastic events, described by the narrator with journalistic restraint, takes place in Pan Kai's puberty:

...al sorprender [el padre] al muchacho curvado hacia adelante sobre el resto de su cuerpo sentado en el piso, en un despliegue sorprendente de elasticidad, el miembro erecto en la boca, la cabeza subiendo y bajando y trazando pequeños círculos en el aire, hasta que se produjo la explosión seminal que lo hizo rebotar hacia atrás enroscándose sobre sí mismo en medio de violentos espasmos que lo sacudían haciéndolo rodar sobre el suelo como una gran bola hasta estrellarse contra la pared y ponerse a llorar del dolor. Después habría de ver claramente como su hijo se enderezaba, se ponía en pie trastabillando y escupía una mezcla de semen y sangre de la que, sobre el piso de madera, brotaban pequeños botones que enseguida se abrían formando diminutas violetas (Ibid. 37-38).

...when he [his father] surprised the boy [who was] curved forward over the rest of his body, seated on the floor, in a suprising display of elasticity, his erect member in his mouth, his head moving up and down and tracing small circles in the air, until the seminal explosion was produced that bounced him backwards twisting him around himself in the midst of violent spasms that shook him, making him roll along the floor like a large ball until he smashed against the wall and began to weep with pain. Afterward, he would see clearly how his son straightened himself out, got to his feet staggering and spat out a mixture of semen and blood from which, on the wooden floor, sprang small blossoms which immediately opened, forming tiny violets.

Pan Kai never becomes alarmed by these improbable episodes which have taken place since his childhood because "éstos y otros fenómenos se repitieron en forma sostenida a lo largo de los años y porque, quizá por eso mismo, estaba convencido de que se trataba simplemente de acontecimientos naturales" ("these and other phenomena were repeated continually through the years and because, perhaps for that very reason, he was convinced that it was simply a matter of natural events") (Ibid. 38).

The autoerotic scene at the end of which violets are formed is so impossible to accept as having occurred in the real world, that the reader feels obliged to to look for a symbolic, transcendent meaning which, of course, does not negate the fantastic level of the magician's personal life.

There are three major elements in this scene: solitude, eroticism and creation. A boy, different from other boys, instead of being in the company of friends, is alone. He is too young to be able to satisfy his sexual urges with girls, but his sexual impulses --(pro)creative impulses-- are so imperative that he manages to carry out a form of masturbation as convincing for this fictional character as it is improbable for the reader. And this self-insemination, although it produces no son, does produce flowers.

The narrator relates these events with detachment, almost journalistically, accepting them as unusual but not supernatural. Pan Kai believes they are perfectly normal. The attitude of the implied author and the reactions of the protagonist place the story within the realm of magic realism. However, the reader is incapable of accepting this account literally, as with other improbable (for the reader) moments in the private life of the magician, moments that are always brief, profound and intimate. For this reason, we feel it incumbent upon us to search for a metaphoric meaning in this scene.

The most basic elements we have are these: someone is carrying out a process that is solitary --absolutely solitary-- and from this activity, to which he contributes his blood, which is to say, his life, and his semen, the seeds of his posterity, there are produced --not without pain-- flowers, which is to say, beauty. These elements --solitary activity, a certain degree of suffering, devotion to life, the posterity and beauty of the product-- inevitably makes us think of artistic-literary creation.

We have to admit that artistic creation resembles masturbation more than coitus. It is a solitary activity in which the performer communes, for the duration of the activity, not with another person, but with him/herself. The poet delves deep within his/her own being without taking into account the desires and sensibilities of other persons. Only the commercial artist, the commercialized writer, so to speak, produces for a specific audience; the legitimate artist does not think about these matters. The writer surrenders to the most personal, most intimate fantasies imaginable. He/she suffers "birth pangs" upon finishing the work, and after the literary or artistic work is finished experiences something akin to post partum depression.

Of course, the fruit of the artistic labor is not the flesh and blood offspring, the continuation of corporeal life, but something less common, more aesthetic, something that permits the artist to express him/herself, to unburden him/herself and which, a posteriori, may establish links with those who appreciate the work of art.

The short story, "El agua" ("Water"), so long (twenty-seven pages), so filled with the events of an entire lifetime, so realistic at times, so fantastic at bottom, is an extended metaphor representing the men and women who devote their lives exclusively to art, who sacrifice themselves on the altar of artistic creativity, even at the expense of family life, becoming solitary beings. This sacrifice turns the artist into a unique and more authentic creator. The solitude of the artist, the doing without a family of one's own combined with singularity of purpose and dedication to one's calling also results in the artistic profession's resembling a sort of priesthood.[81] In this context, the father of the pubescent Edwin Pan Kai is a witness, a voyeur who --like the audience of an artistic performance or simple entertainment, like the reader of literary works-- suprised and incredulous, glimpses the artist's world.

The somewhat shorter story, "Luna de miel" ("Honeymoon") --an ironic title because it seems more like a "luna de hiel" ("bitter moon") — deals with a couple who arrive at a resort to enjoy their honeymoon. The only way of reaching the town or leaving it is by boat. The hotel, and, in fact, the entire town, appear to be deserted, but the honeymooners believe, or want to believe, that it only seems deserted because the townfolk retire early.

The atmosphere becomes increasingly strange. After a nap, from which they are awakened by intense heat, they receive the impression that "el tiempo no transcurría" ("time was not passing") (*Ahora*, 84). There is still no sign of a living soul. They go back to sleep, but upon waking, the man notices that his wife is missing. Looking out the window, he fleetingly sees her running along the beach. He puts his bathing suit on and, after noting with alarm that there is still no one at the reception desk but that the key to room number 13, the room next to the honeymoon couple's, is in its cubbyhole, goes out to search for his wife. She has disappeared, and the husband, after spending the entire day trying to find her, returns to the hotel in a state of desperation.

As he arrives at his room, he sees that the door of the adjacent room, number 13, is open. Impelled by curiosity, the man walks in. The door closes and a voice thunders, "los estábamos esperando" ("we were waiting for you"). There is no one in the room, but this deep, rough voice loudly commands him to be seated. The narrator comments, "Más solo que nunca, de pie en el centro de la estancia generada por alguna alucinación que me incluía, tuve la convicción, no obstante, de que aquello era una excrescencia de la realidad" ("More alone than ever, standing in the middle of the room generated by some hallucination that included me, I was convinced, nevertheless, that all that was an excrescence of reality") (Ibid. 89). "Siéntese" ("Sit down"), the ownerless voice insists, and the narrator complies.

The voice orders him to undress, and the narrators obeys. At this point, a different voice, a voice described as "un poco menos honda y quebrada, aunque más vibrátil" ("somewhat less deep, less rough, although more vibrant"), declares: "queremos su semen" ("we want your semen").

Bewildered, the narrator stammers something, and the new voice insists, "semen." The narrator, intimidated by the voices, masturbates, trembling. He feels degraded and, at the same time, as though he were outside of reality. What follows is so bizarre that it merits quoting exactly:

> Cuando al fin exploté --extraño orgasmo carente de placer-- vi claramente como las ráfagas desaparecían en el aire, muy cerca de su origen, entubadas por una fuerza invisible. Como absorbidas por un goloso imán, acechante, cuya existencia estaba más allá de toda comprensión razonable (Ibid. 90).

> When I finally exploded --a strange orgasm devoid of pleasure-- I saw clearly how the spurts disappeared into the air, very close to their origin, consumed by an invisible force. As though absorbed by a greedy magnet, lying in wait, whose existence was beyond all reasonable comprehension.

Later, after suffering nausea and terrible heat, he awakens in bed in his own room, longing for his wife who is nowhere to be found. It has become obvious that the narrator is actually the only person present in the hotel. He knocks on the door of room number 13, the room in which he had --or dreamed he had-- the uncanny experience. The door opens inward. On the floor in the middle of the room is a bundle. He approaches it and opens the blanket in which it is wrapped, uncovering a child's face that stares at him "desde el óvalo perfecto de la cara" ("from the perfect oval of its face") with eyes described as "neutros, fríos" ("indifferent, cold").

Of course, it is possible to enjoy this story as a narration of pure fantasy, like one of those television plays in Rod Serling's series "The Twilight Zone" in which everything is possible and nothing needs to be explained rationally --in the present case, a question of perhaps supernatural or extraterrestrial forces or ectoplasm in search of some minimal embodiment. Nevertheless, in view of our previous examination of the short story, "El agua" ("Water"), it is possible to conceptualize what is happening in "Luna de miel" as another metaphor --highly extended, of course-- of artistic creation. The artist is obliged to do without his wife, to sacrifice his personal life, to give up his happiness, while engaging in the solitary act of creation.

As in the story "El agua," and for similar reasons, the symbol of artistic creation --an autoerotic task carried out in solitude-- is masturbation. Furthermore, since art reflects only certain elements of reality, an incomplete part of reality, we find the bodiless head of a child as emblematic of the reflection of partial reality. The "voice" that commands the narrator to give up his semen, and which might be assumed to have jealously frightened his wife away in order to demand his complete attention, represents the voice --just as mysterious, just as powerful and just as demanding-- of artistic inspiration.

The Narrator of the very short story, "El punto de referencia" ("The Point of Reference"), Who speaks from the point of view of the first person, turns out to be God. We discover this as we read the monologue in which the Narrator mentions His reasons for having created life. The story takes place after the destruction of the human race. The first sentence of this two-page narrative reads, "De nada sirvió esa torpe evolución de siglos" ("That clumsy centuries-long evolution served no purpose") (Ibid. 7). The second sentence affirms that "el germen del fracaso estaba ya en la primera idea" ("the germ of failure was already present in the original idea").

The Narrator explains this affirmation in greater detail; basically, the explanation is that through "experiencia tras experiencia, cada vez más refinada" ("experiment after experiment, one more refined than the previous"), the Narrator --God-- offered a challenge to human beings without looking ahead to the possible results, simply by giving them the capacity of reaching the limit, their maximal human and scientific potential (Ibid. 8). This is why human ambition grew and man tried to reach limitless power.

This human desire to advance, to progress, to succeed and to become greater --a desire implanted by the Creator from the beginning-- is what led to the catastrophe alluded to, to self-destruction, perhaps through a nuclear war. This is why God-the-Narrator states: "Ahora me corroe la culpa y floto en un limbo de soledades infinitas más terrible que el vacío" ("Now I am consumed with guilt and I float in a Limbo of infinite solitude more terrible than the void") (Ibid.).

The Narrator informs us that "la vida vuelve a ser inexistente fuera de mí" ("life is once more inexistent outside of Myself") (Ibid. 7). Toward the end He admits:

> Sé, como lo sé todo, que siempre será necesario, fuera de mí, un punto de referencia. Claro que podría crear nuevos entes negándoles ahora toda voluntad propia, intuiciones agudas y toda posibilidad de aprendizaje a partir de la memoria (Ibid. 8).

> I know, as I know everything, that a point of reference, outside of Myself, will always be necessary. Of course I could create new beings, this time denying them any will of their own, any insight and any possibility of learning starting with memory.

He continues to struggle with the possibilities and ends by thinking, "debo decidir de qué manera llenar mi soledad" ("I must decide how to fill my solitude"). Then He wonders, "Pero...¿y si vuelvo a equivocarme?" ("But... what if I make another mistake?") (Ibid.).

This exceedingly short story is filled with philosophical, theological and metaphysical suggestion. We encounter the problems of free will, of human nature, and even of the nature of God. In this story the Creator is not a perfect being, but one capable of making errors, something He discovers too late. Neither is this God the biblical Father of the human family, but rather a scientist who by means of scientific experiments attempts to perfect His inventions, and even destroys them and has to decide whether to renew them or simply admit defeat. This piece of fiction, within the highly restricted confines of a two-page short story, includes very serious speculations about the universe, man and God. It could even be thought of as a metaphysical text. At the same time, however, this story is yet another metaphor of artistic creation and destruction.

This would not be the first time that the writer has been portrayed as a god who creates his own world. Neither is there anything new in conceptualizing God as the Author of existence. But in this short piece Jaramillo Levi presents us with a God who, like a novelist dissatisfied with the drafts of his novel, is at the point of deciding whether the work deserves to be redeemed through modification and change, or if the novel is so bad that it is irredeemable and merits destruction.

This God creates the world and life because He needs "un punto de referencia" ("a point of reference") external to Himself, and also to "llenar mi soledad" ("to fill my solitude") (Ibid. p. 8). Within the context of the other short stories examined above, Jaramillo Levi suggests that the writer practices his vocation in order to aleviate a certain sense of solitude, of isolation, of loneliness. Thus, paradoxically, we see that the writer, or any creator, isolates him/herself from contact with society, turns in on him/herself, in order to create his/her own world. But, to what end? It turns out that the artist takes on this solitary work precisely for the purpose of aleviating his/her solitude, and to locate, to find him/herself within that world, to discover his/her point of reference in the fictional characters the artist creates.

What Jaramillo Levi suggests is that the creative artist feels alone in the company of his/her fellows until the artist locks him/herself away for a while with the creatures of the writer's own world, of the world the writer invents. In other words, the artist needs to return to the sources of his/her own being, needs to be with the products of his/her imagination, in order to feel whole. And, like the God presented to us in "El punto de referencia," the writer must destroy drafts, and think and rethink the work until either perfecting it or destroying it.

One of the themes concealed beneath the surface of Enrique Jaramillo Levi's fiction --that surface which can be by turns fantastic, uncanny or magically real and often grotesque-- is closely related with artistic creation, literary creation. Even in narratives as different in plot and tone as "El agua," "Luna de miel," and "Punto de referencia," we find extended metaphors of the creative process in which auto-eroticism often symbolizes this process and solitude always play a causal or essential part.

WORK CONSULTED

Jaramillo Levi, Enrique. *Ahora que soy él*. San José (Costa Rica): Editorial Costa Rica, 1985.

NOTES

1. Uslar Pietri's term was "mundo americano," which literally means "American world." However, the use of "América" and "americano" among Latin American intellectuals is very different from the use of "America" and "American" in English. In English the terms are inexact but convenient terms for the United States and the adjective referring to our country. In Spanish it refers to all the Americas -- North and South-- in opposition to Europe, with a concentration, more often than not, on Latin America, stressing the inclusion of the Native ("Indian") and African elements that make the Americas different from Europe.

2. Todorov's term, translated into English as "the uncanny," in the original French is "l'étrange," literally, 'the strange.'

3. The German expression used by Freud equivalent to the English "the uncanny" is das Unheimliche, *Imago*, 5 (1919), quoted in Chanady, p. 4. The German term, it should be noted, literally translates as the "un-homey," "un-homelike" and therefore, "unfamiliar."

4. For a more complete treatment of this topic, see Joseph L. Henderson, in Carl G. Jung, *Man and His Symbols* (Garden City, N.Y.: Doubleday & Co., 1964), p. 125. For a treatment of one of these themes in literature see Clark M. Zlotchew, *Libido into Literature: The "Primera Época" of Benito Pérez Galdós*, (San Bernardino: Borgo Press, 1993), pp. 91-98.

5. Nahualism is the belief, as delineated by Miguel Ángel Asturias in *Hombres de maíz*, that each person has his/her nahual, an animal closely associated with him/her and into which h/she can change. According to J.E.S. Thompson, it is an extremely important belief in Central America. The association is thought to be so close between a man and his nahual, according to Thompson, that if a man's nahual is shot in the leg, a similar wound will appear on the man's leg (p. 24).

6. Assuming the reader and the author do not really share the mind

set of the implied author and the characters. If they were to share this "primitive" mentality, the work of fiction would not be magic realism for them; it would be simply realism.

7. A useful translation of this essay is "Narrative Art and Magic," in *Borges, a Reader: A Selection from the Writings of Jorge Luis Borges.*

8. "Hearing the Scream," *Atlas: A Window on the World*, December 14, 1967, p. 58, quoted (in Spanish) by Bautista Gutiérrez, p. 25. (My translation into English. I have not been able to see the original.)

9. In this context it is interesting to note that Borges declares that, before he writes a short story, he "receives" a "modest revelation" in which the beginning and the end of the story are given to him; he then invents the middle. See Zlotchew, "Entrevista con Jorge Luis Borges," 153 (in Spanish) and Zlotchew, *Voices of the River Plate*, p. 36 (in English translation).

10. For a full treatment of Borges' unknowing involvement with Shih Huang Ti and with the artist Norman Daly as instruments of an archetype which destroys the past and builds the future, see Zlotchew, "Tlon, Llhuros..."

11. For an account of Borges' reading, with the aid of a German-English dictionary, Heinrich Heine's *The Book of Songs*, and this exercise leading to his learning sufficient German to read, in the original German, Mayrink's *Der Golem*, see Pickenhayn, 20.

12. Borges confesses that he did not realize, certainly did not intend, that when he wrote the poem "El Gólem" he was utilizing the same plot as that of the story "Las ruinas circulares." An American student in Texas pointed out this affinity to him, an affinity Borges recognized as genuine. See Sorrentino, p. 35.

13. Borges' *Obra poética 1923-1966* (one of the volumes of the *Obras completas* of Borges published by Emecé in 1964) contains, besides the collection, *El otro, el mismo*, the collections *Fervor de Buenos Aires, Luna de enfrente,, Cuaderno San Martín, Para las seis cuerdas* y *Museo. El otro, el mismo*, was published separately (but including *Para las seis cuerdas y Museo*) by Emecé in 1969 and 1970.

14. These quotations represent FitzGerald's third, fourth and fifth (i.e. definitive) versions of the poem, quatrains 68 and 69. In his first version, this thought appears in quatrains 46 and 49, in which he writes: "For in and out, above, about, below,/'Tis nothing but a Magic Shadow-show,/Play'd in a Box whose Candle is the Sun,/Round which we Phantom Figures come and go./ ... "Tis all a Chequer-Board of Nights and Days/Where Destiny with Men for Pieces plays:/Hither and thither moves, and mates, and slays./ And one by one back in the Closet lays." FitzGerald, pp. 34-35.
FitzGerald's second version, quatrains 73 and 74, reads: "We are no other than a moving row/Of visionary Shapes that come and go/Round with this Sun-illumin'd Lantern held/In Midnight by the Master of the Show:/Impotent Pieces of the Game he plays/Upon this Chequer-Board of Nights and Days;/Hither and thither moves, and checks, and slays,/And one by one back in the Closet lays." FitzGerald, pp. 87-88.

15. Marco Denevi seems to share these ideas. Cf. the narrator's words referring to the relationship between Cecilia Engelhard and Leonides Arrufat in *Ceremonia secreta*: "...todo formaba parte de una vasta ceremonia, todo integraba uno de esos intrincados mecanismos de los que nunca sabremos quién es el relojero, si Dios o nosotros."('...everything formed part of a vast ceremony, everything formed one of those intricate mechanisms of which we never will know who the watchmaker is, whether it is God or ourselves.')

16. Loewenthal is German for "Valley of Lions," and the lion is the king of beasts.

17. My translation, as are all subsequent translations of Borges. The original Spanish reads: "fortuita conjunción de un astrónomo persa que condescendió a la poesía, de un inglés excéntrico que recorre, tal vez sin entenderlos del todo, libros orientales e hispánicos, surge un extraordinario poeta, que no se parece a los dos."

18. See James Irby's Introduction to Jorge Luis Borges, *Other Inquisitions 1937-1952*, p. iv.

19. The Emperor had exiled his own mother because he considered

her a libertine, but the orthodox (those who followed the canonical books) felt his behavior was impious.

20. According to my off-the-record conversation with Borges at Allegheny College, Meadville, PA, June 1985.

21. Norman Daly, in a letter to me dated June 21, 1973, stated that he had heard of Borges, but had not read "Tlon, Uqbar, Orbis Tertius."

22. The exhibit appeared at museums in Akron, Ohio (September, 1972), Rochester, N.Y. (November, 1972), Albany, N.Y. (January, 1973), and was scheduled to open in Indianapolis, Indiana and Binghamton, N.Y. at later dates, according to Daly's letter.

23. In this regard, Borges' method of writing a short story is interesting. He claims he "receives" the beginning and the end of a short story in a "very modest revelation," and then has to fill in the middle. See Zlotchew, *Voices of the River Plate: Interviews with Writers of Argentina and Uruguay* (San Bernardino: Borgo Press, p. 36.

24. These devices were discussed by Borges during his lecture of September 2, 1949 and are applied to Borges' own work by Emir Rodríguez Monegal in "Jorge Luis Borges y la literatura fantástica," *Número*, vol. 1, no. 5 (November-December 1949), 448-455. A synopsis of the lecture was provided by Carlos Alberto Passos in *El País* (Montevideo, Uruguay), September 3, 1949.

25. "Spanish American Fantasy and the `Believable, Autonomous World'" *International Fiction Review*, vol. 1, no. 1 (1974), 5.

26. Bruce Morrissette reports that Gide, in his *Journal* of 1893, describes the procedure as "a `mise en abyme'('throwing into an abyss, or a bottomless pit') or 'mise en place'('putting in place') in the center of a work another version of the subject `on the scale of the characters.'" (My translation from French) *Les Romans de Robbe-Grillet,* Preface de Roland Barthes, nouvelle édition augmentée (Paris: Les éditions de Minuit, 1963), note 4, p. 117. (The French edition is here cited rather than the revised and expanded English translation because the details included in the above quote are not included in the English version.) See also Morrissette, "Un Héritage d'André

Gide: La Duplication intérieur, "*Comparative Literature Studies,* vol. 7, no. 2 (June 1971), 125-42.

27. "Un Héritage d'André Gide: La Duplication intérieur," *Comparative Literature Studies,* 7, 2 (June 1971), 130. (My translation from French, as are all other quotations from Morrisette, Ricardou and Robbe-Grillet.)

28. Quoted by Morrissette in "Un Héritage..," 137-38.

29. Cf. "Robbe-Grillet's penchant for miniature imitations of the work which are written into the work itself, such as the 'légende de l'ile' ('Legend of the Island'), which sums up the story of Mathias in [the novel] *Le Voyeur,* or the painting of a café scene which illustrates the soldier's situation in [the novel] *Dans le Labyrinthe (In the Labyrinth)*..." Morrissette, *Les Romans de Robbe-Grillet* (see note 2), note 4, p. 117. (The French edition is used here again, in my translation, because details there included are excluded from the English version.)

30. Morrissette, "Un Héritage..., " 130. For an article partly concerning the significance of the "native song," see Leo Bersani, "Toward an Esthetic of Disappearance? Narrative Murder, in *Balzac to Beckett: Center and Circumference in French Fiction* (New York: Oxford University Press, 1970), pp. 272-299.

31. See, e.g., Morrissette, *The Novels of Robbe-Grillet,* translated from the French, revised, updated, and expanded, with a Foreword by Roland Barthes (Ithaca and London: Cornell University Press, 1975), p. 52.

32. *Discusión* (Buenos Aires: Emecé Editores, 1964), p. 91. (My translation from Spanish, as are all subsequent quotations from Borges)

33. There is in this phenomenon a similarity to Robbe-Grillet's novel *Les Gommes (The Erasers).* An oversimplified summary of the basic plot of "The Secret Miracle" would be almost identical with the resumé actually provided by Robbe-Grillet for *The Erasers* in the "priere d'inserer": "Car le livre est justement le récit des vingt-quatre heures qui s'écoulent entre ce coup de pistolet et cette mort, le temps

que la balle a mis pour parcourir trois ou quatre metres --vingt-quatre heures 'en trop'." ("Because the book is precisely the account of the twenty-four hours that elapse between this gun being fired and this death, the time the bullet took to cover three or four meters --twenty-four hours too long.")

The extra twenty-four hours are dramatically reinforced in *The Erasers* by the detective's watch stopping at the exact time the hit man fires at Dupont (7:30 P.M.) only starting again after the victim is actually killed twenty-four hours later. It is impossible to overlook the striking resemblance between this fact and the clock's striking seven in "Los enemigos" ("The Enemies"), the summary of Hladík's play within Borges' short story "El milagro secreto" ("The Secret Miracle") at the beginning of the play and then again at the end.

34. Original Spanish: Este drama observaba las unidades de tiempo, de lugar y de acción; transcurría en Hradcany, en la biblioteca del barón de Roemerstadt, en una de las últimas tardes del siglo diecinueve. En la primera escena del primer acto, un desconocido visita a Rooemerstadt. (Un reloj da las siete, una vehemencia de último sol exalta los cristales, el aire trae una apasionada y reconocible música húngara.) A esta visita siguen otras; Roemerstadt no conoce las personas que lo importunan, pero tiene la incómoda impresión de haberlos visto ya, tal vez en un sueño. Todos exageradamente lo halagan, pero es notorio --primero para los espectadores del drama, luego para el mismo barón-- que son enemigos secretos, conjurados para perderlo. Roemerstadt logra detener o burlar sus complejas intrigas; en el diálogo, aluden a su novia, Julia de Weidenau, y a un tal Jaroslav Kubin, que alguna vez la importunó con su amor. Éste, ahora, se ha enloquecido y cree ser Roemerstadt... Los peligros arrecian; Roemerstadt, al cabo del segundo acto, se ve en la obligación de matar a un conspirador. Empieza el tercer acto, el último. Crecen gradualmente las incoherencias: vuelven actores que parecían descartados ya de la trama, vuelve, por un instante, el hombre matado por Roemerstadt. Alguien hace notar que no ha atardecido: el reloj da las siete, en los altos cristales reverbera el sol occidental, el aire trae una apasionada música húngara. Aparece el primer interlocutor y repite las palabras que pronunció en la primera escena del primer acto. Roemerstadtd fle habla sin asombro; el espectador entiende que Roemerstadt es el miserable Jaroslav Kubin. El drama no ha ocurrido: es el delirio circular que interminablemente

vive y revive Kubin." The English is my translation, as are all subsequent English versions of quotations from this book.

35. Borges' synopsis of Hladík's play is only one paragraph long since, according to Borges, it was included in the story mainly, though not entirely, for the purpose of lending verisimilitude to "The Secret Miracle": "Of course, I couldn't say that Hladík had thought out a drama or a work of art and say nothing whatever about it. Because then, of course, that would fall flat, I had to make it convincing." Burgin, p. 38.

36. "Nous devons enfin nous garder des constructions allégoriques et du symbolisme" ('We should keep away from allegorical constructions and from symbolism') Morrissette quoting Robbe-Grillet, p. 23.

37. "En autorisant les objets a fonctionner comme supports ou soutiens des passions (autre facon de dire qu'ils son des correlatifs objectifs), Robbe-Grillet acceptait une concession nécessaire" ('By allowing objects to function as supports or reinforcements for the passions (another way of saying they are objective correlatives), Robbe-Grillet was making a necessary concession') Morrissette, p. 32.

38. There is an article that partially refers to the significance of the mysterious "native song" in *La Jalousie*. See Leo Bersani, "Toward an Esthetic of Disappearance? Narrative Murder," in *Balzac to Beckett: Center and Circumference in French Fiction* (New York: Oxford University Press, 1970), pp. 272-99.

39. See note 3 above.

40. I spoke with Robbe-Grillet at the Mid-America Conference on Hispanic Literature, Washington University, Saint Louis, Missouri, October 27-29, 1988.

41. Original Spanish: "No, nunca pensé en escribir novelas. Yo creo que si yo empezara a escribir una novela, yo me daría cuenta de que se trata de una tontería y que no la llevaría hasta el fin. Posiblemente esto sea una invención de mi haraganería. Pero creo que Conrad y Kipling han demostrado que un cuento corto --no demasiado corto--,

lo que podríamos llamar long short story, puede contener todo lo que contiene una novela, con menos fatiga para el lector." In Sorrentino, *Siete conversaciones con Jorge Luis Borges*, p. 112.

42. Original Spanish: "Desvarío laborioso y empobrecedor el de componer vastos libros, el de explayar en quinientas páginas una idea cuya perfecta exposición oral cabe en pocos minutos. Mejor procedimiento es simular que esos libros ya existen y ofrecer un resumen, un comentario... Más razonable, más inepto, más haragán, he preferido la escritura de notas sobre libros imaginarios."

43. My translation into English, as will be all subsequent translations.

44. Cf. the vision which is "empapada de poesia y magia" ('drenched in poetry and magic'). Fernando Aínsa, *Tiempo reconquistado* (Montevideo: Ediciones Géminis, 1978), p. 185.

45. Note, however, the naive summary on the back cover of Julio Ricci, *Ocho modelos de felicidad* (Buenos Aires: Macondo Ediciones, 1980): "También aquí aparecen algunas figuras de la Europa Oriental con sus caídas en un raro tipo de absurdismo y de grotesco, desconocido entre los latinos del Río de Plata" ('Here too appear figures from Eastern Europe with their falling into a strange form of the absurd and the grotesque, unknown among the Latins of the River Plate').

46. "La carta" has been published, in my English translation, as "The Letter," in *Webster Review*, 10, 2 (Fall 1985), 40-46, and in *Falling Through the Cracks: Stories of Julio Ricci*.

47. "Además, una polaca era para mí una gran mujer. No era como una alemana o una francesa o una italiana" Ricci, *Cuentos*, p. 128. ('Besides, a Polish woman was something special, something grand, in my estimation. She was different from a German woman or a French woman or an Italian woman'). *Falling...*, p. 33.

48. Contrary to popular stereotypes, González adds that the greys of Poland conceal a great human warmth, while the shamelessness of the bright and ardent sun and of the immodest light of the Mediterranean lands mask a fundamental coldness (*Cuentos*, p. 130;

Falling, p. 35). This idea bears a startling resemblance to that expressed by the protagonist of Thomas Mann's "Tonio Kroger." Cf. "I'm fed up with Italy... the whole belleza business makes me nervous. All those frightfully animated people down there with their black animal-like eyes; I don't like them either. These Romance peoples have no soul in their eyes. No, I'm going to take a trip to Denmark." Thomas Mann, *Death In Venice and Seven Other Stories*, trans. by H. T. Lowe-Porter, Vintage Books, a Division of Random House (New York: Alfred A. Knopf, 1936), pp. 106-107.

49. "El shoijet," has been translated into English twice. In my translation, under the title, "Old Friends," it appears in my collection of Ricci stories, *Falling Through the Cracks*, pp. 61-73. In Miriam Varon's translation, titled "The Shoyhet," it has the distinction of being the only piece written by a non-Jew in an anthology of Latin American writings of Jewish theme. See Robert and Roberta Kalechofsky, general editors, *Echad: An Anthology of Latin American Jewish Writings*, pp. 113-21.

50. "[I]nexplicable"; "secretos" (p. 22); "raro" ('strange'); "lo desconocido" ('the unknown'); "secreta" (p. 23); "mágico"; "inasible" ('ungraspable') (p.24); "impenetrables" ('unfathomable') (p. 26).

51. The most recent book to speak of the blood libel is Paul Johnson, *A History of the Jews* (New York: Harper and Row, 1987), pp. 310, 322, 357, 571, 577.
For an entire book dealing exclusively with the infamous blood libel trial of twentieth-century Russia, see Maurice Samuel, *Blood Accusation: The Strange History of the Beilis Case* (New York: Alfred A. Knopf, 1964).
For accusations against Jews of ritual murder through the ages, see.g., Max L. Margolis and Alexander Marx, *A History of the Jewish People* (Philadelphia: The Jewish Publication Society of America, 1927), pp. 367-68, 380-82, 384-85, 389-90, 375, 376, 417-18, 541, 542-44, 579-81, 651-53, 674, 685, 693, 700, 716-17. The blood accusations which occurred in the nineteenth century are referred to between pages 651 and 700, while the infamous Beilis trial of the twentieth century is covered on pp. 716-17.
See also Heinrich Graetz, *History of the Jews*, 6 vols. (Philadelphia: The Jewish Publication Society of America, 1898), Vol III, pp. 378-81, 402,

499, 564, 583-85, 591, 635-37, 643; Vol. IV, pp. 223-24, 227, 246-47, 261-64, 298-307, 545-50; Vol. V, pp. 45-49, 174-77, 185-88, 279-87, 633-42, 650, 654-55, 661-62, 669. (Twentieth century cases do not appear in Graetz because it was published before those cases took place.)

52. In many quarters this suspicion subsist even today. Although seemingly incredible, these blood libels are with us even today. In 1989 *Response* reported that the church of San Domenichino de Marina di Massa (Italy) commemorates, annually in the month of August, the supposed crucifixion, stabbing and bleeding to death of a five-year-old Christian child, Domenichino (Dominguito) de Val, by Jews in the year 1250 in Zaragoza, Spain. At the annual event, this church distributes a booklet that presents as true the story --with emotional language and horrifying details-- of the supposed ritual murder of this child allegedly committed by the Jewish community of Zaragoza in order to fulfill some Jewish ritual. This church also sponsors an annual poetry contest concerning the ritual murder. In 1989 this competition attracted 3,000 participants who came from every part of the world. See *Response*, 10, 2 (September 1989), 1-2.
In June 1990 it was reported that London police were trying to find the authors of a leaflet, *Snides of March*, which accused Jews of ritually killing Christian children. The flyer was sent to members of the British Parliament and had been distributed at universities. See *Dateline World Jewry*, June 1990, 7.
A *Newsweek* reporter writes that in the Basilica of Saint Mary of Sandomierz, Poland, "a huge painting" entitled "Infanticide" is displayed. It depicts a group of caricatured Jews who kidnap, stab and dismember Christian babies as part of a religious rite. The explanatory plaque claims that members of the Jewish community murdered two babies in Sandomierz in 1698 and in 1710 respectively. The reporter, in April 1990 --the end of the twentieth century-- asked a passing nun if the Jews really did all that. She answered, "Of course. They used to do those things in the past, but not now. There are no more Jews left in Poland." See Tom Mathews, "The Long Shadow," *Newsweek*, 115m 19 (May 7, 1990), 43.
Also in 1990, 846 years after the first trial against the Jews of Norwich, England for ritual murder, the blood libel arose again, this time in the United States. Jacob Wetterling, a St. Cloud, Minnesota child, disappeared. The police investigating the case were also trying to find the origin of the posters and flyers that blamed the

disappearance of the twelve-year old boy on alleged Jewish "ritual murder." See *Response*, 11,2 (May 1990), 15.
As is well known, not only is murder against Jewish law, but so is the ingestion of blood, even that coming from animals acceptable for food, which humans beings are not. Human sacrifice is also explicitly forbidden.

53. Lázaro's mother is "muy simpática" ('very likeable') (G, p. 23), and later his daughter is also "muy simpática" (p. 28). Lázaro, after death, is "el querido shoijet" ('the dear shoyhet') (p. 33).

54. In general terms, Ricci has said: "Autobiography can be found in all writers. Some authors distance themselves a great deal from what might appear to be autobiographical, or else they drown it, they cover it up, they hide it in some manner. But I have no prejudice against utilizing autobiographical elements." Zlotchew, *Voices*, p. 86. Original Spanish: "Yo diría que io autobiográfico está en casi todos los autores. Algunos se alejan mucho de lo que parece ser autobiográfico.... Pero yo no tengo ningún prejuicio en utilizar elementos autobiográficos" Zlotchew, *Discurso*, 85.
More to the point is a statement of Ricci's that provides an autobiographical basis for the short story "El Shoijet" ("Old Friends"): "Cuando tenía catorce años me reunía con un amigo judío ruso, Lázaro Jalfín o Halfin, gran amigo con quien pasábamos horas jugando. Y él estudiaba hebreo y yo estudiaba con él" (Ibid., p. 79.) ('When I was fourteen years old, I used to get together with a Russian-Jewish friend, Lázaro Jalfín or Halfin, a great friend I spent hours with at play. And he was studying Hebrew, and I would study with him'). For details on Ricci's languages, and for slightly edited version of the preceding statement, see Zlotchew, *Voices*, pp. 81-82.
Even more specificaliy, Ricci provides an autobiographical explanation for the peculiarly reticent behavior of the protagonist of "El Shoijet" ("Old Friends"): "Era por el año 32, la época de la Depresión. Luego no lo vi mas [a Lázaro Halfin]. Pero un día, cuando [yo] andaba por el Centro, lo reconocí, ya un hombre de casi sesenta años, parado en la puerta de un negocio de platería. Quise hablarle, pero no me atreví. Me faltó fuerza, y no lo vi más en la platería" ('It was around 1932, the era of the Depression. Then I didn't see him [Lázaro Halfin] any more. But one day, when I was walking around downtown, I recognized him, now an almost sixty-year old

man, standing in the doorway of a silversmith's shop. I wanted to talk to him, but I didn't have the nerve. I couldn't get myself to do it, and I didn't see him at the silversmith's after that') From Julio Ricci's letter to me of July 6, 1985.

55. The counting of money (and, therefore, the stereotype) was eliminated in Varon's English version, "The Shoyhet," where, instead, one reads: "I imagined the Jewish proprietor combining, with old knowledgeability, business and religion, traits from the east joined without friction." In *Echad*...p. 117.

56. Lázaro's grandfather, a rabbi, appears to have come from some kind of temple or "lugar sagrado" ('holy place') in which then reigns serenity, respect and austerity, as well as "grandeza de espíritu y el amor por todo lo desconocido" ('greatness of spirit and a love for all that is unknown') (*Grongo*, p. 23; *Falling*, p. 63). The synagogues contain an impressive austerity and seriousness, and the ark holding the Torah possesses a simple nobility and grandeur which López finds indescribable (*Falling*, p. 65; *Grongo*, p. 25.)

57. Uruguayans and Argentineans seem to think of Europeans as parsimonious. The Hungarian of Ricci's "Las ideas parsimoniosas del Señor F. Szomogy" is an extreme example (*Ocho modelos*, pp. 11 -39). Cf. the Argentinean satirist, Fernando Sorrentino, in the short story "En defensa propia": the Hofers, Europeans (vaguely, either German, Austrian or Swiss) living in Argentina, have exchanged extravagantly costly gifts with the narrator's native-born Argentinean family, yet the narrator's wife, displeased because her latest gift is not as expensive as those received by her husband and son, says: Estos Hofer, como buenos europeos, son unos tacaños (my emphasis). Sorrentino, *En defensa propia*, p. 123. For my English version of this story, see, "In Self Defense," *Webster Review*, 9, 1 (Spring 1984), 87-83.

58. For editorial purposes, the words in brackets were deleted from *Voices of the River Plate*.

59. The original title, "El shoijet," contains the Spanish transliteration of the Hebrew word for the ritual animal slaughterer of kosher meat. My translation of this story uses the title "Old Friends."

60. "Pero el escritor que, naturalmente, es la clave para mí de toda esa literatura [de los escritores centro-europeos y rusos en general, de los que más influencia han tenido en mis gustos y en mi sensibilidad] es Kafka, lógicamente. Sí, Kafka." See Zlotchew, "Entrevista con Julio Ricci", 81. ('But the writer who, naturally, is for me the key to all that literature [of Central European and Russian writers in general, of those who have had the most influence on my tastes and on my sensibilities] is Kafka, logically. Yes, Kafka.') For the English version of the full interview with Ricci, see Zlotchew, *Voices of the River Plate*, pp. 77-92. For the above statement specifically (somewhat modified by editing, see p. 83.

61. The exercise of absolute and arbitrary power results in the deification of the members of the Board ("Directorio" or "Superioridad"): "pero parece que los humanos sienten un placer divino en entregarse a esa actividad [desjerarquizar a un individuo]" ('but it seems that humans feel a divine pleasure in giving themselves over to that activity [demoting someone from executive to underling]' (my emphasis), CC, p. 23).

62. Note, however, the naively biased summary on the back cover of *Ocho modelos de felicidad*" "También aquí aparecen algunas figuras de la Europa Oriental con sus caídas en un raro tipo de absurdismo y de grotesco, desconocido entre los latinos del Río de la Plata" ('Here too appear some characters from Eastern Europe with their tumbles into a weird brand of the absurd and the grotesque, unknown among the Latins of the River Plate').

63. For a full discussion of this theme in Spanish, see Zlotchew, "Europa en la ficción...", and in English, "Utopian Escapism..."

64. See note 5 above.

65. See footnote 5 above.

66. "El shoijet," translated into English by Miriam Varón under the title "The Shoyhet," has the distinction of being the only piece written by a non-Jew in an anthology of Latin American writings on Jewish themes. See Kalechovsky, gen. editors, *Echad...*, pp. 113-121. A different English version is "Old Friends" translated by Zlotchew in

Ricci, *Falling...*, pp. 61-73.

67. Terms that mean: 'inexplicable'; 'secrets' (G, 22); 'strange'; 'the unknown'; 'secret' (G, 23; 'magical'; 'ungraspable' (G, 24; 'unfathomable' (G, 26).

68. Blood libels (accusations of ritual murder) against the Jews are well documented. See, for example, Max L. Margolis and Alexander Marx, *A History...*, passim. The Middle Ages were rife with these accusations. For the blood libels that took place during the more enlightened nineteenth-century, see pages 651 and 700. For the infamous Beilis case of our own twentieth century in Russia, see pp. 716-17.
Also see Heinrich Graetz, *History...*, passim. The Beilis case does not appear in Graetz because this work was published before the trial occurred.
See too Paul Johnson, *A History...*, pp. 310; 322; 357; 571; 577.
For a book that deals exclusively, and in detail, with the twentieth-century Beilis case, see Maurice Samuel, *Blood...*

69. Although seemingly incredible, these blood libels are with us even today. In 1989 *Response* reported that the church of San Domenichino de Marina di Massa (Italy) commemorates, annually in the month of August, the supposed crucifixion, stabbing and bleeding to death of a five-year-old Christian child, Domenichino (Dominguito) de Val, by Jews in the year 1250 in Zaragoza, Spain. At the annual event, this church distributes a booklet that presents as true the story --with emotional language and horrifying details-- of the supposed ritual murder of this child allegedly committed by the Jewish community of Zaragoza in order to fulfill some Jewish ritual. This church also sponsors an annual poetry contest concerning the ritual murder. In 1989 this competition attracted 3,000 participants who came from every part of the world. See *Response*, 10, 2 (September 1989), 1-2.
In June 1990 it was reported that London police were trying to find the authors of a leaflet, *Snides of March*, which accused Jews of ritually killing Christian children. The flyer was sent to members of the British Parliament and had been distributed at universities. See *Dateline World Jewry*, June 1990, 7.
A *Newsweek* reporter writes that in the Basilica of Saint Mary of

Sandomierz, Poland, "a huge painting" entitled "Infanticide" is displayed. It depicts a group of caricatured Jews who kidnap, stab and dismember Christian babies as part of a religious rite. The explanatory plaque claims that members of the Jewish communityh murdered two babies in Sandomierz in 1698 and in 1710 respectively. The reporter, in April 1990 --the end of the twentieth century-- asked a passing nun if the Jews really did all that. She answered, "Of course. They used to do those things in the past, but not now. There are no more Jews left in Poland." See Tom Mathews, "The Long Shadow," *Newsweek*, 115m 19 (May 7, 1990), 43.

Also in 1990, 846 years after the first trial against the Jews of Norwich, England for ritual murder, the blood libel arose again, this time in the United States. Jacob Wetterling, a St. Cloud, Minnesota child, disappeared. The police investigating the case were also trying to find the origin of the posters and flyers that blamed the disappearance of the twelve-year old boy on alleged Jewish "ritual murder." See *Response*, 11,2 (May 1990), 15.

As is well known, not only is murder against Jewish law, but so is the ingestion of blood, even that coming from animals acceptable for food, which humans beings are not. Human sacrifice is also explicitly forbidden.

70. Lázaro's mother is "muy simpática" ('very likeable') (G, 23), and further on her daughter too is "muy simpática" (G, 28). Lázaro Dorón, deceased, is "el querido shoijet" ('the beloved shoyhet') (G, 33).

71. In general terms, Ricci said, "Lo autobiográfico está en casi todos los autores. Algunos se alejan mucho de lo que parece ser autobiográfico... Pero yo no tengo ningún prejucio en utilizar elementos autobiográficos." In Zlotchew, "Entrevista con Julio Ricci," 85. "Autobiography can be found in all writers. Some authors distance themselves a great deal from what appears to be autobiographical... But I have no prejudice against using autobiographical elements." In Zlotchew, *Voices...*, 86.

More specifically with relation to "Old Friends," he said, "De muchacho...me reunía con un amigo judío ruso, Lázaro Jalfín o Halfin, el que estudiaba hebreo, y yo estudiaba con él. Pasábamos horas jugando. Era durante la Depresión... Luego no lo vi más, pero un día, hace 6 años, cuando [yo] andaba por el centro [de

Montevideo], lo reconocí, ya un hombre de casi 60 años, parado en la puerta de un negocio de platería. Quise hablarle, pero no me atreví. Me faltó fuerza, y no lo vi más. Mi cuento, 'El shoijet', está basado en esto." Composite of my oral interview with Ricci in 1984 (about studying Hebrew) and information in Ricci's letter to me of July 6, l985 (about seeing Lázaro but not speaking to him). In edited form in Zlotchew, "Entrevista...," p. 79. (As a boy I would get together with a Russian-Jewish friend named Lázaro Jalfín or Halfin, who was studying Hebrew, and I would study with him. We would play for hours. It was during the Depression.... Then I didn't see him any more, but one day, about six years ago, as I was walking downtown [in Montevideo], I recognized him, now a man of almost sixty, standing in the doorway of a silversmith's shop. I wanted to speak to him, but I didn't have the courage. I couldn't get up my nerve, and I never saw him again. My short story, 'El shoijet' ['Old Friends'] is based on this.") A much edited (shortened) reference to Lázaro Halfin is made in Zlotchew, *Voices...*, p. 82.

72. It is well known that ecstasy in communion with God was the goal sought after by the Spanish mystics of the sixteenth century. The prose of Saint Theresa of Avila and the poetry of Saint John of the Cross, for example, contain descriptions of the ecstasy they experienced. Cf. "El [poeta] místico describe psicológicamente sus propias experiencias del éxtasis..." ('The mystic [poet] describes psychologically his/her own experiences of ecstasy...') In Ángel del Río, *Historia...*, p. 255.

73. Aniela Jaffe insists that the process of individuation frequently is symbolized by a voyage of discovery to unknown lands. She provides as literary examples John Bunyan's *Pilgrim's Progress* and the "traveler" of Dante's *Divine Comedy*. For the narrator of "Old Friends" the Jewish ambiences are definitely unknown lands through which he journeys on a voyage of discovery.

74. In a woman's psyche, of course, the Self assumes femenine personifications.

75. See note 13 above.

76. My English translation, as are all subsequent quotations from

Identidad. Because the Spanish word vela means both 'candle' and 'sail,' and because Manuel Fernando intuits that they are about to embark for the Indies (on a ship with sails), and because Brailovsky declared that he liked to play with the idea that one could read the future in another's eyes (Zlotchew, *Voices*, p. 66), I took liberties with the translation of this passage, in an attempt to reproduce the double charge, in the present context, that the Spanish word vela bears in the original text.

77. Original Spanish: "Así pasó un tiempo que entonces no pudo medir y después ya no importaba, pero que se le antojó un solo día inmenso, compuesto por infinitos fragmentos de cabalgatas sedientas, bajo un cielo chato y bajo, en el que brillaban varios soles simultáneos, sobre un fondo de azul intenso, casi negro, como los ojos abiertos de los caídos, que se quedaban absorbiéndolo, allí, olvidados por la tropa que continuaba su marcha interminable, en ese día único, colosal, en el que habían nacido en la la llanura, clavados a sus caballos para siempre." (pp. 219-20).

78. My interviews with the writers were held in Spanish. *Voices...* contains my English translation of them.

79. John Burdon Sanderson Haldane, *Possible Worlds* (1927), quoted in *Bartlett's Familiar Quotations*, p. 683.

80. The collection, *Ahora que soy él*, compact and suggestive, consists of thirteen short stories (the author subtitled the book: *13 cuentos en contra* (*13 Short Stories Against*). The author's other collections of short stories include: *Catalepsia* (*Catalepsy*) (Panama: 1965); *Duplicaciones* (*Duplications*) (Mexico City: 1973; 1982); *El buho que dejó de latir* (*The Owl that Stopped Throbbing*) (Mexico City: 1974); *Renuncia al tiempo* (*Renunciation of Time*) (Mexico City: 1975); and two anthologies of his own work: *Caja de resonancias: 21 cuentos fantásticos* (*Sound Box: 21 Fantastic Stories*) (Mexico City: 1983) and *La voz despalabrada* (*The Voice Without Words*) (Costa Rica: 1986). Jaramillo Levi has also published several collections of poetry including: *Los atardeceres de la memoria* (*Nightfalls Remembered*) (Mexico City: 1978); *Fugas y engranajes* (*Fleeing and Connecting*) (Mexico City: 1982); *Cuerpos amándose en el espejo* (*Bodies Making Love in the Mirror*) (Mexico City: 1982) and *Extravíos* (*Misplacements*) (Costa Rica: 1989).

81. Rubén Darío, the most important of the writers of the Latin American Modernist movement (late nineteenth, early twentieth centuries), often conceives the poet as a priest, a prophet, an intermediary between ordinary mortals and the divine.

www.ingramcontent.com/pod-product-compliance
Lightning Source LLC
Chambersburg PA
CBHW021811220426
43662CB00006B/262